A Landscape Preservation Bibliography

INTRODUCTION

Since the publication of *Preserving Historic Landscapes* by the National Park Service in 1990, the field of landscape preservation has witnessed a dramatic increase in project work and academic interest. These developments have fueled the profession, and can be measured by the increased number of books, technical publications, journal articles and conferences on the subject. However, readers are often challenged by conflicting approaches in landscape preservation literature, practice and policy, and interpretations of the *Secretary of the Interior's Standards.*

Additionally, there is a growing number of articles in allied disciplines, such as archaeology, cultural geography, anthropology, natural sciences, and computer technology which may not be known or easily obtained by landscape architects and preservation planners engaged in project work today.

Recognizing that the National Park Service mission includes *"a wise use of our land, (and) preserving the environmental and cultural values of our national parks and historical places,"* this document has been prepared to guide the user in obtaining practical guidance to make educated decisions when researching, planning, managing and undertaking project work in cultural landscape resources.

Making Educated Decisions: A Landscape Preservation Bibliography has been conceived and designed for use by practitioners (landscape architects, horticulturists, architects, planners, archaeologists); stewards (administrators and managers of historic parks and gardens, national parks and forests, state historic preservation offices, municipalities, not-for-profit organizations, advocacy groups, professional associations); as well as educators, scholars and students.

The bibliography contains over five hundred annotated citations referenced by subject, author and geographic indices. The project database has been generated using ProCite bibliographic software, with a commitment to its continued maintenance and ultimate availability to the public in the future.

W0007120

Making Educated Decisions

The bibliography includes English language publications, with a predominant focus on landscape preservation philosophy, research, preservation planning, practice, treatment, management and maintenance. These techniques are often represented in the form of illustrated case studies. In all, forty-eight states and twenty-seven countries are represented.

Literature from diverse disciplines has been included. Bibliographic entries were chosen from books, scholarly journals, technical reports, and published conference proceedings--with each citation critically evaluated for compatibility with the *Secretary of the Interior's Standards*. Papers from conference proceedings have been noted in a single citation. In all cases, resources cited are publicly available.

This publication does not include unpublished master's and doctoral theses, literature in languages other than English, or historical literature not involving landscape preservation. Such publications are more readily available, captured in other bibliographies, and routinely included in educational curricula. Although recent Cultural Landscape Reports are certainly of interest, they are often not readily available and have also not been included, although many citations present and discuss their methodologies and research findings.

The bibliography is organized alphabetically by author, but can be searched by subject, author, or location utilizing the indices at the back of the book.

Finally, *Making Educated Decisions* requires an ongoing commitment if it is to remain current. It is our hope that readers who utilize this publication will bring books and articles to our attention in the future. These can be submitted to the National Park Service Preservation Assistance Division for inclusion in the database and later updates to this publication. .

Charles A. Birnbaum, ASLA and Cheryl Wagner
September 1994

ACKNOWLEDGEMENTS

Charles Birnbaum and Cheryl Wagner participated in all phases of the project. In addition, many others offered steady support.

Several local and regional institutions supported the research for this bibliography. They are: the Arnold Arboretum; Dumbarton Oaks Studies in Landscape Architecture; Loeb Library, Harvard University Graduate School of Design; the Horticulture Library of the Smithsonian Institution; the National Trust for Historic Preservation, Washington, D.C., and the University of Maryland's National Trust Library.

Many dedicated librarians were of invaluable assistance. Special thanks go to Phyllis Anderson (Arnold Arboretum); Annie Day Thacher and Linda Lott (Dumbarton Oaks Garden Library); Mary Daniels (Loeb Library, Harvard Graduate School of Design); Marca L. Woodhams and Paula McClosky (Smithsonian Horticulture Library), and Sally Sims Stokes, Karen Nelson, and Sarah Miranda (University of Maryland, National Trust Library).

For invaluable assistance in developing our subject index, special thanks to Marca L. Woodhams for generously sharing her Archives of American Gardens Subject Authority, and to Sally Sims Stokes for similarly sharing her customized Index Terms List.

Gary Hilderbrand, Department of Landscape Architecture, Harvard Graduate School of Design, helped establish the conceptual framework for the project.

Without Jean Jones' extraordinary research and organizational skills, dedication and good humor, the project would not have been realized.

The research phase was assisted by Phyllis Anderson, Sally S. Boasberg, JoAnn Lawson, and Paul Daniel Marriot.

An able team of volunteers helped annotate the literature cited. They are: Phyllis Anderson, Sally S. Boasberg, Lee D'Zmura, John and Kathleen Kay, Paul Daniel Marriott, Christopher Shaheen, and Piera Weiss.

Making Educated Decisions

Making Educated Decisions

Technical support came from many sources. Lawrence F. Karr's computer expertise made the project possible. In addition, Karen Nelson generously consulted on Pro-Cite. The technical support staff at Personal Bibliographic Software, Inc., Ann Arbor, Mich., were also invaluable.

National Park Service, Preservation Assistance Division staff H. Ward Jandl, Kay Weeks, Michael Auer, Theresa Robinson, and Carol Gould all were involved. Special thanks to Kimberly Konrad for producing the Geographic Index and Robert R. Page from the Park Historic Architecture Division who assisted with production.

CONTENTS

Citations

1. Abbott, Stanley. "Historic Preservation: Perpetuation of Scenes Where History Becomes Real." *Landscape Architecture* 40, no.4 (1950): pp.153-157.

    Historic perspective toward preserving national, state, county parks and reservations (e.g. battlefields, fortifications, formal parks, historic villages, house sites, ruins). Management approaches and visitor services. Many National Park Service examples. illus.

2. Adams, William Hampton. "Landscape Archaeology, Landscape History, and the American Farmstead." *Historical Archaeology* 24, no.4 (1990): pp.92-101.

    Rural archaeology, "central place theory," discussed. Author regards examination of the farm within context of landscape history, beyond just house and yard. Farm as microcosm of broad societal changes. illus.

3. Ahern, Katherine. "Visitor Wear and Tear of Cultural Landscapes: Recommendations for Stonehenge." *CRM* 14, no.6 (1991): pp.24-26.

    One of four case studies in 1988 English Heritage examination of visitor use impact on World Heritage Sites. Monitoring use and treatment prescription to reunite Stonehenge with its landscape. Quantitative analysis of uses: peak, daily, monthly, etc. Implications of findings. illus.

4. Ahern, Katherine; Blythe, Leslie H. and; Page, Robert R., eds. "Cultural Landscape Bibliography: An Annotated Bibliography on Resources in the National Park System." Washington D.C.: Park Historic Architecture Division, Cultural Landscape Program, Washington Office, 1992.

    A variety of reports since 1940--over 100 studies for seventy parks organized by National Park Service Region. Chronological and park indices. bib. illus.

5. Ahern, Katherine; Wimble, Andrew. "Wear and Tear at Stonehenge." *Landscape Design* no.194 (Oct.'90): pp.46-48.

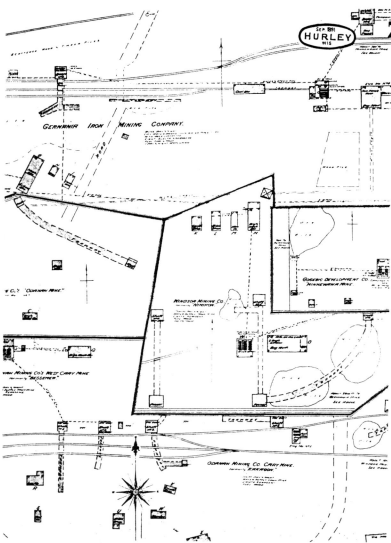

See citation 9: Arnold R. Alanen. "Documenting the Physical and
Social Characteristics of Mining and Resource-Based Communities."
APT Bulletin, 1979. Though originally intended for fire insurance
purposes, Sanborn-Perris maps provided detailed information on the
major commercial, industrial, and public structures in a community;
mining buildings such as these by Hurley, Wis., also were
delineated.

Visitor impact on turf areas at Stonehenge. Grass varieties, periods of high use, visitor circulation, and 'rest periods' for turf outlined. illus.

6.   Aitchison, J. W.; Hughes, E. J. "Commons, Conservation and Amenity in Wales." *Landscape Research* 11, no.3 (1986): pp.17-22.

Legislative and management history of the Common Lands of England and Wales. Strategies for balancing their scenic, cultural and ecological qualities through integrated land management. bib. illus.

7.   Akerman, James B. "Eleutherian Mills Garden Site." *Historical Archaeology* 2, (1968): pp.69-72.

Archaeological survey of early nineteenth century original U.S. home of Eleuthere Irenee du Pont near Wilmington, Del. Magnetometer and resistometer used to help locate garden features. Grass discoloration in visible patterns during dry August field work successfully reveals former garden paths. illus.

8.   Alanen, Arnold R. "Considering Cultural Landscapes." *Historic Preservation Forum* 5, no.1 (1991): pp.20-23.

Discussion of five types of cultural landscapes as defined by the National Park Service: historic scenes, historic sites, designed landscapes, historic vernacular landscapes, ethnographic landscapes. bib. illus.

9.   Alanen, Arnold R. "Documenting the Physical and Social Characteristics of Mining and Resource-Based Communities." *APT Bulletin* 11, no.4 (1979): pp.49-68.

Cultural geographer's description of a dozen types of documentary sources used to develop seven typologies of Mich., Minn., Wis., mining communities. How landscape architects' historic roles are assessed. bib. illus.

10.   Alanen, Arnold R. "Grounded in Reality." *Courier* 34, no.8 (1989): pp.10-13.

Preservation treatment options for management, protection of vernacular landscapes. illus.

11. Alesch, Richard J. "Cultural Landscaping: Buffalo National River." *CRM* 9, no.4 (1986): pp.7-9.

Management Plan overview for Boxley Valley, Ark., by the National Park Service. Balancing natural and cultural issues.

12. Anderson, Timothy G. "Czech-Catholic Cemeteries in East-Central Texas: Material Culture and Ethnicity in Seven Rural Communities." *Material Culture* 25, no.3 (1993): pp.1-18.

European, Catholic, Protestant influences. Marker form, spatial orientation, native language incidence, maintenance, discussed. bib. illus.

13. Andropogon Associates, Ltd. *Earthworks Landscape Management Manual.*, U.S. Department of the Interior National Park Service Park Historic Architecture Division. Cultural Resources, Washington, D.C., 1989.

Management strategies and interpretive guidelines to resolve conflicts between preservation requirements and visitor impact on earthwork sites. Applicable to both natural and cultural landscapes. Includes guidelines of generic solutions. bib. illus.

14. Andrus, Patrick W. *Guidelines for Identifying, Evaluating, and Registering America's Historic Battlefields.*, U.S. Department of the Interior. National Park Service Cultural Resources. Interagency Resources Division., Washington, D.C., 1992. 27 pp.

Historical perspective and current status. Rationale for battlefield preservation. Guidance for successful preparation of nominations. Definitions and types. Mapping, field work, setting boundaries, documentation and assessment techniques. Step-by-step process for determining integrity and significance. bib. illus.

15. Anfield, John. "Sustainable Tourism in the Nature and National Parks of Europe." *The George Wright Forum* 10, no.4 (1993): pp.87-94.

International park conservation and tourism organizations collaborate and categorize protected areas, develop guidelines. Case study: Dovedale, Peak National Park, U.K. bib. illus.

16. Anthony, John. "Identifying the Surviving Elements of the Layout." *Garden History* 3, no.4 (1975): pp.27-34.

Overview of elements used in gardens (walls, hedges, water features, etc.) from sixteenth to nineteenth century; Cites need for comprehensive U.K. survey of historic landscapes and gardens. illus.

17. Austin, Richard L., Coordinating ed.; Kane, Thomas, J.; Melnick, Robert Z.; Turner, Suzanne Louise, Contributing eds. "The Yearbook of Landscape Architecture Historic Preservation." New York, New York: Van Nostrand Reinhold Company, 1983.

Twenty articles on the theory, philosophy, and implementation of landscape preservation work in the US. Papers include: Introduction: Landscape Architecture and Historic Preservation, Robert Z. Melnick; Landscape Research: Keeping Faith with Today and Tomorrow, Catherine M. Howett; An Invitation to Landscape Interpretation, Ann L. Marston; Listening to the Historic Landscape: Economy in Image-making, Suzanne Turner; Historic Plants for Historic Gardens, Ann Leighton; Native Vegetation Restoration: Another Route to the Past, Darrell Morrison; Urban Design: Catalyst for Comprehensive Revitalization, Richard Macias; Historic Preservation as Applied to Urban Parks, Patricia M. O'Donnell; Commercial Streetscapes, Steve McNiel; The Memory of War: Reflections on Battlefield Preservation, Reuben M. Rainey; Common Sense: Guidelines for Greens, Thomas Paine; Magic Markers, Kenneth I. Helphand; Conservation Planning Along an Historic Corridor, Kerry J. Dawson; New Center Neighborhood Revitalization, Johnson, Johnson, Roy, Inc.; Community-based Preservation in Amana Colonies, Timothy and Genevieve Keller; The Magnolia Mound Plantation, Unicorn Studios; A Living-history Farm: The Buckley Homestead, Charles F. Lehman and Janice A. Cervelli, LeRoy Troyer and Associates; Landscape Preservation and Our Agricultural Heritage, Joseph S. R. Volpe; Back Bay Fens, Carol R. Johnson and Associates, Inc.;

Val-Kill: The Eleanor Roosevelt National Historic Site, Kane and Carruth, P.C.; and, Black Settlements in America, Entourage, Inc. illus.

18. Badenoch, Teresa S. "Wilhelmshohe: A Unique Record of a Changing Landscape by J.H. Muntz (1786-1796)." *Journal of Garden History* 6, no.1 (1986): pp.50-61.

Nineteen extant sepia and black ink drawings accompanied by written descriptions done by J.H. Muntz constitute valuable documentation for evolution of late-eighteenth century German garden. bib., annotated. illus.

19. Barkhof, H.; Oldenburger-Ebbers, C. S. "Plants for the Restoration of the Baroque Garden of the Palace of the Loo at Apeldoorn." *Journal of Garden History* 1, no.4 (1981): pp.293-304.

Report of the Working Party for Garden Design regarding construction of parterres and plantings for restoration of seventeenth century Baroque pleasure garden. bib. illus.

20. Barthold, Elizabeth. "Documenting Historic Parks in the Nation's Capital." *CRM* 14, no.6 (1991): pp.7-9.

Two-year Historic American Building Survey (HABS) documentation of L'Enfant (1791)/McMillan (1902) plan for Washington, D.C. Park furniture, plantings, vistas, existing conditions recorded. Use of National Register's Integrated Preservation Software (IPS). Preparation for National Historic Landmark nomination. illus.

21. Batey, Mavis. "The Swiss Garden, Old Warden, Bedfordshire." *Garden History* 3, no.4 (1975): pp.40-43.

First historic garden restoration funded under the U.K.'s Clause 12 of the Town and County Amenities Act of 1974. The Swiss Garden, 1829, believed to be inspired by J.B. Papworth's "Hints on Ornamental Gardening."

22. Battaglia, David H. *The Impact of the Americans With Disabilities Act on Historic Structures.*, National Trust for Historic Preservation, Washington, D.C., 1991. 16 pp.

Types of facilities covered under law, necessary actions, enforcement, time frame. Case studies: Frank Lloyd Wright Home and Studio, Oak Park, Ill.; Drayton Hall, Charleston, S.C.; Chesterwood, Stockbridge, Mass.; Colonial Williamsburg, Williamburg, Va.; Frelinghuysen Arboretum, Morristown, N.J.; and, Cape May Point Lighthouse, Maine. Focus on structures. Selected resource list. bib., annotated. illus.

23. Beasley, Ellen. *Reviewing New Construction Projects in Historic Areas.*, National Trust for Historic Preservation, Washington, D.C., 1992. 24 pp.

Outline of the basic documents and procedures essential to public design review for new construction projects in historic districts. Focus on the design of new buildings for "historic settings." National examples. bib. illus.

24. Beaty, Laura. "How Well is the National Park Service Managing its Cultural Resources: The NPCA Point of View." *Public Historian* 9, no.2 (1987): pp.125-134.

National Parks and Conservation Association (NCPA) perspective on definition and management of cultural resources; internal and external influences on National Park Service (NPS) mission; relationship between U.S. Department of the Interior and the NPS; role of constituents in policy planning.

25. Beaumont, Constance Epton. "Historic Preservation and Growth Management." *Historic Preservation Forum* 6, no.3 (1992): pp.35-40.

Local land use planning techniques, such as growth management or zoning must be considered if historic preservation is to be successful. bib.

26. Beaumont, Constance Epton. "Property Rights and Civic Responsibilities." *Historic Preservation Forum* 7, no.4 (1993): pp.30-35.

Preservation is a philosophy that can be applied broadly to improve our communities; property rights do not necessarily conflict with preservation values. bib.

27. Beckett, Penny; Dempster, Paul. "Birkenhead Park" *Landscape Design* No.185, (1989): 24-29.

Current landscape preservation planning efforts for Liverpool, U.K. park, in decline for decades. illus.

28. Bell, Robert D. "Archaeology and the Rococo Garden: The Restoration at Painswick House, Gloucestershire." *Garden History* 21, no.1 (1993): pp.24-45.

Analysis of existing paintings and confirmation of their details through extensive archaeology. Assessment of accuracy of contemporary records of earliest known gothic revival garden structures before 1748. bib. illus.

29. Bell, Robert D. "The Discovery of a Buried Georgian Garden in Bath." *Garden History* 18, no.1 (1990): pp.1-21.

Archaeology, analysis and reconstruction of a town garden. Implications of discoveries for other sites. bib. illus.

30. Bennett, John; Barrett, Brenda; Cooley, Randall; Dunbar, Keith B. "The America's Industrial Heritage Project." *Trends* 29, no.2 (1992): pp.31-34.

South-western Pa. Heritage Preservation Commission's project to commemorate industrial development, 1800-1945. Preservation and managment of resources; emphasis on tourism and development. Products: "Reconaissance Survey of Western Pennsylvania's Road and Sites," 1985, "Action Plan," 1987. Role of the National Park Service and HABS/HAER documentation project.

31. Berg, Jeffrey; Powell, John L. "Lighting Historic Landscapes." *APT Bulletin* 9, no.3 (1989): pp.10-12.

Balancing history and modern illumination function in historic landscapes. Historic background, small and large scale examples in urban areas and parks in N.Y.C., N.Y., and Cambridge, Mass. Sources. illus.

32. Berg, Shary Page. "Approaches to Landscape Preservation Treatment at Mount Auburn Cemetery." *APT Bulletin* 24, no.3&4 (1992): pp.52-58.

See citation 32: Shary Page Berg. "Approaches to Landscape Preservation Treatment at Mount Auburn Cemetery." *APT Bulletin*, 1992. This image circa 1870 illustrates the ornamental or gardenesque period at Mount Auburn with circular fountain, fine turf, bedding plants and scattered trees.

Historical background of U.S. rural cemetery movement. Analysis and treatment strategies for the nation's oldest resource of its type, Cambridge, Mass. bib. illus.

33. Berg, Shary Page. "Fairsted: Documenting and Preserving a Historic Landscape." *APT Bulletin* 20, no.1 (1988): pp.40-49.

   Brookline, Mass., home and office of Frederick Law Olmsted. Preservation and management plan and implementation since 1980 National Park Service acquisition. Discussion of research methodology. Chronology shown in four plan views. bib. illus.

34. Berg, Shary Page. "The Nation's Oldest Rural Cemetery: Mount Auburn, Cambridge." *CRM* 16, no.4 (1993): pp.17-19.

   Historic context, research, inventory, analysis, findings. Rational for rehabilitation for selected treatment. illus.

35. Berg, Shary Page. "Rescuing Fairsted." *Landscape Architecture* 77, no.4 (1987): pp.83-85.

   Transforming the Olmsted firm office into a landscape architectural museum. Preserving buildings, landscape, archives. National Park Service acquisition (1979), public opening (1981). Collections overview. bib. illus.

36. Birnbaum, Charles A. "The End of the Period for Period Landscapes." *Historic Preservation News* 33, no. 6 (1993): p.6.

   Calls for recognition of layered chronology of historic landscapes in preservation planning, resulting in rehabilitation and preservation becoming primary treatments for most sites; less often restoration, reconstruction.

37. Birnbaum, Charles A. *Landscape Composition Preservation Treatment: Defining an Ethic for Designed Landscapes.*, National Association for Olmsted Parks, Bethesda, Maryland, 1992. 14 pp.

   Response to NAOP Workbook 2 [see Toth, Edward]. Emphasis on research, integrity analysis and understanding design intent when rehabilitating a park's plant materials.

Review of the preservation planning process emphasizes vegetation management. Case studies: Meadowport Arch, Prospect Park, Brooklyn, N.Y.; and Polly Pond, Downing Park, Newburgh, N.Y. bib. illus.

38. Birnbaum, Charles A. "Landscape Preservation Today." *Historic Preservation Forum* 7, no.3 (1993): pp.6-15.

General discussion of landscape preservation developments over past decade. National initiatives, research and reference aids, archives, training and technical assistance, education, project work, grants, legislative opportunities. bib. illus.

39. Birnbaum, Charles A., ed. The Landscape Universe: Historic Designed Landscape in Context., Armor Hall at Wave Hill, Bronx, New York, 23 April, 1993. United States: The Catalog of Landscape Records at Wave Hill in conjunction with the National Park Service, Preservation Assistance Division, 1993. 113 pp.

Papers included: Defining the Landscape Universe, Charles A. Birnbaum; A Look at the Naturalist Designs of Jens Jensen and the Preservation of Lincoln Memorial Garden, Springfield, Illinois, Robert E. Grese; The Olmsted Brothers' Residential Communities: A Preview of a Career Legacy, Arleyn A. Levee; Selecting Rehabilitation as a Treatment for the Olmsted Brothers' Designed Hills and Dales Park, Dayton, Ohio, Noel Dorsey Vernon; Andre Parmentier: A Bridge Between Europe and America, Cynthia Zaitzevsky; Cultural Landscape Analysis The Vanderbilt Estate at Hyde Park, New York, Patricia M. O'Donnell; Gateway to the Past: Establishing a Landscapes Context for the National Register, Linda Flint McClelland; Understanding the Bigger Picture for Chicago's Historic Parks, Julia Sniderman; Landmarks of Landscape Architecture: The Historical Context for National Park Service Landscape Architecture, Ethan Carr. bib. illus.

40. Birnbaum, Charles A. "Making Educated Decisions on the Treatment of Historic Landscapes." *APT Bulletin* 24, no.3&4 (1992): pp.42-51.

Explanation, applications of the draft 'Guidelines for the Treatment of Historic Landscapes.' Illustrated examples. bib. illus.

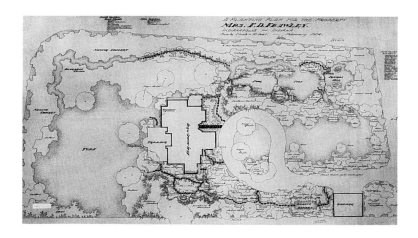

See citation 39: "A Look at the Naturalist Designs of Jens Jensen and the Preservation of Lincoln Memorial Garden, Springfield, Illinois" by Robert E. Grese. Included in *The Landscape Universe: Historic Designed Landscape in Context*, 1993. Jensen's planting philosophies for the Lincoln Memorial Garden (top) can be gleaned from his earlier work such as this planting plan for Mrs. F.D. Frawley.

41. Birnbaum, Charles A. *Protecting Cultural Landscapes: Planning, Treatment and Management of Historic Landscapes.*, U.S. Department of the Interior. National Park Service Cultural Resources. Preservation Assistance Division., Washington, D.C., (1994): 20 pp.

    Background and definitions. Step-by-step process for preserving historic designed and vernacular landscapes. A framework and guidance for undertaking project work to ensure a balance between historic preservation and change. Research, inventory, documentation, period plans, historic plant inventory, archaeology, analysis, treatment, interpretation, maintenance and implementation. bib. illus.

42. Birnbaum, Charles A. "A Reality Check for Our Nation's Parks." *CRM* 16, no.4 (1993): pp.1,3-4.

    Introduction to thematic issue: establishing context, planning and implementing treatment work. Application of draft 'Guidelines for the Treatment of Historic Landscapes.' bib. illus.

43. Birnbaum, Charles A. "Volunteers: A Resource for Park Stewardship." *Landscape Architecture* 83, no.3 (1993): pp.58-59.

    Strategies for citizen participation in park preservation. Overview of national and state programs (e.g. work release, adopt-a-monument). Examples: Emerald Necklace Parks, Boston, Mass., Central Park, N.Y.C., N.Y., Prospect Park, Brooklyn, N.Y., Downing Park, Newburgh, N.Y. illus.

44. Birnbaum, Charles A.; Park, Sharon C. "Maintaining Integrity: Accessibility and Historic Landscapes." *Landscape Architecture* 83, no.6 (1993): p.144.

    Integrity evaluations guide accessibility solutions in historic landscapes. Case studies: Rancho Los Alamitos, Long Beach, Calif., Eugene and Carlotta O'Neill House, Danville, Calif., Morningside Park, N.Y.C., N.Y., Arnold Arboretum, Jamaica Plain, Mass. illus.

45. Birnbaum, Charles A.; Crowder, Lisa E., eds. "Pioneers of American Landscape Design: An Annotated Bibliography."

Washington, D.C.: U.S. Department of the Interior, National Park Service, Cultural Resources, Preservation Assistance Division, Historic Landscape Initiative, 1993.

Sixty-one biographical profiles. Nearly 1,200 bibliographic citations with location and description of archival collection contents. Introduction relates research to treatment work. illus. 144 pp.

46.   Birnbaum, Charles A.; Page, Robert R., eds. "Thematic Issue on Landscape Interpretation." *CRM* 17, no.7 (1994): pp.2-4, 47-48.

Introductory paper suggests new directions for cultural landscape interpretation. Overview of trends gleaned from thirteen author contributions from the U.S., U.K., Australia and Poland. bib. illus.

47.   Bisschop, Gerard Roosegaarde. "Dutch Country Seats Considered as Historic Monuments: an Attempt at Legal Protection of Gardens and Parks." *Journal of Garden History* 1, no.4 (1981): pp.345-352.

Difficulties in applying the Monuments Act to Dutch country seats as a first attempt at protecting large landscapes containing both buildings and gardens and/or parks designed as a single entity. bib. illus.

48.   Blackwell, Charles W.; Childers, Gary D. "Chickasaw Cultural Preservation." *Trends* 29, no.2 (1992): pp.35-37.

Protection of Chickasaw Indian culture in northwestern Miss. Archaeological discovery of a major village at a proposed development site. Confirmed presence of human bones, artifacts, resulting in cataloging, non-invasive study, protection and reinterment at a new fifteen acre site.

49.   Bomberger, Bruce D. "PA SHPO Inventories French and Indian War Sites." *CRM* 16, no.10 (1993): pp.13-15.

Pennsylvania's Bureau of Historic Preservation receives National Park Service funding for preliminary survey, mapping methodology for mid-eighteenth century sites. Findings, implications.

See citation 54: Elizabeth Brabec. "Tomorrow's Parks and Open
Spaces Preservation: Strategy for Waterford Village." *CRM*, 1993.
The rural landscape of Waterford, Va. is part of a growing
community. The relationship of road, field, hedgerow and viewshed
are important to the character of its historic landscape.

50. Booth, Edmund. "How the Planning System Could Help."
     Landscape Research 7, no.1 (1982): pp.31-32.

     Need to inventory and survey historic extant U.K. gardens
     and parklands to raise awareness and guide management.
     Benefits, limitations of Tree Preservation Orders. Need to
     educate planning profession. bib.

51. Borchers, Perry E. "Photogrammetry's Use in Fixing
     Scenes." *Landscape Architecture* 66, no.3 (1976): pp.270-275.

     Documenting southwestern historic landscapes. illus.

52. Bourke, Max. "How Will My Garden Grow? A Philosophy
     for the Restoration of Historic Gardens." *Journal of Garden
     History* 3, no.1 (1983): pp.49-54.

     Author asserts that slight modifications are needed to use
     1964 ICOMOS Venice Charter for worldwide applications of
     an historic preservation ethic for restoration of historic
     gardens. bib.

53. Boyles, Fred. "Historic Landscaping: Moores Creek National
     Battlefield." *CRM* 9, no.4 (1986): pp.9-10.

     Restoration treatment of battlefield vegetation based on
     research findings. illus.

54. Brabec, Elizabeth. "Tomorrow's Parks and Open Spaces
     Preservation: Strategy for Waterford Village." *CRM* 16, no.4
     (1993): pp.20-22.

     The application of the draft 'Guidelines for the Treatment of
     Historic Landscapes' to rural Va., National Historic
     Landmark. Land owner cooperation and prioritizing areas for
     protection. bib.

55. Bradford, J. White; Roddewig, Richard J. "Preparing a
     Historic Preservation Plan." Chicago, Illinois: American
     Planning Association, 1994.bib. illus.

56. Bratton, Susan, ed. Vegetation Change and Historic
     Landscape Management: Proceedings of the Conference on
     Science in the National Parks., Colorado State University, Fort

Collins, Colorado, 13-18 July 1986. The George Wright
Society and the U.S. National Park Service, 1988. 214 pp.

Towards a Future for National Park Service Research: The
1986 Conference on Science in the National Parks, Raymond
Herrmann; The Management of Historic Ecosystems and
Landscapes in National Parks, Susan P. Bratton; Management
of Biotic Cultural Resources, Ian J. W. Firth; Cultural
Landscape Management at Boxley Valley, Buffalo National
River, Richard J. Alesch; The Use of Vegetation Disturbance
History Source Materials: Three Examples from Great Smoky
Mountains National Park, Charlotte Pyle; Landscape Evolution
at San Juan Island National Historical Park, James K. Agee;
Prehistoric Vegetation Changes at Wupatki National
Monument, Arizona, Steven K. Cinnamon; The Impacts of
European Settlement on the Vegetation and Fire Regimes of
Canaveral National Seashore, Florida, Kathryn Davison and
Susan P. Bratton; The Micronutrient Status of Tree Species
Affected by the Lawn Lake Flood, Rocky Mountain National
Park, Colorado, Kenneth A. Barrick and Mark G. Noble;
Landscape History and its Implications for Fire Management
in a Maritime Forest, Buxton Woods, Cape Hatteras National
Seashore, Susan P. Bratton and Kathryn Davison; San Juan
Island National Historical Park Pilot Planting Project, James
F. Milestone; Integrated Pest Management for Historic
Landscapes, Nora J. Mitchell and Deirdre Gibson; Historic
Orchard Management, John Donahue; Native Plant
Revegetation Techniques in the Coastal Environments of
Golden Gate National Recreation Area, James F. Milestone.
bib. illus.

57. Briggs, C. Stephen. "Welch Gardens Under Threat: an
Archaeological Perspective." *Journal of Garden History* 11,
no.4 (1991): pp.199-206.

Suggests that Wales has many examples of gardens from
different periods, but no comprehensive policy for recording
or protecting these resources. bib. illus.

58. Brink, Peter H. "Livable Communities and Historic
Transportation Corridors." *CRM* 16, no.11 (1993): pp.52-53.

Short and long term goals. Approaches to identification and preservation. Outreach and coalition building, e.g. National Trust's Main Street Program and heritage tourism.

59. Brinkley, M. Kent. "Colonial Williamsburg." *Landscape Architect* 10, no.4 (1994): pp.28-33.

Accuracy of 1927 reconstruction discussed in light of contemporary evidence. Impacts of new findings on visitors' experience. illus.

60. Brittenden, J. E. "Surveying for Town Planning by the Use of Aerial Photographs." *The Garden Cities and Town Planning Magazine* 10, no.4 (1920): pp.87-89.

U.K. magazine description of benefits of what was then a new technology. Suggests use of stereoscopic viewers, training for photo-interpreters. illus.

61. Brown, Richard A. "Record-Keeping for Botanic Gardens." *Landscape Architecture* 66, no.3 (1976): pp.265-267.

A computerized inventory of over 120,000 cultivated plants. Case study of Plants Records Center at Longwood Gardens, Kennett Square, Pa. illus.

62. Brown, William E.; Veirs, Stephen D. ,. Jr ,. eds. Partnerships in Stewardship: Proceedings of the Seventh Conference on Research and Resource Management in Parks and on Public Lands., Jacksonville, Florida, 16-20 November 1992. Hancock, Michigan: The George Wright Society, 1993. 479 pp.

Sixty-four papers addressing: Erasing Boundaries; Partnerships in Cultural Resources Research and Management; Wildlife Research and Management: The Example of White-tailed Deer; Air Quality Research and Management: The Example of Ozone; Aquatic Research and Mangement: The Example of Restoration; Techiques for Choosing Research and Management Priorities; Research, Management and Policy in a Long-term Perspective; Looking at Ecosystems; Mandates; The Native Presence in Parks and Wilderness; Emerging Ideas to Build Cooperation and Understanding; Case Studies and Work in Progress. bib.

63. Bryant, Julius. "London's Historic House Parks." *Landscape Design* no.201 (June '91): pp.31-35.

Treatment issues at three historic estates in London, U.K. Management, public involvement, education discussed. illus.

64. Buggey, Susan. "Managing Cultural Landscapes in the Canadian Parks Service." *CRM* 14, no.6 (1991): pp.22-23.

Canadian terminology and definitions. Management policies: value, public benefit, understanding, respect, integrity. Recent work: inventories, research, management policies; legislative impacts. National Park examples. bib. illus.

65. Buggey, Susan; Stewart, John J. "Lakehurst and Beechcroft: Roches Point, Ontario, Canada." *Journal of Garden History* 1, no.2 (1981): pp.147-166.

Assessing the possible influence and evidence for Frederick Law Olmsted, Sr. designs on two Canadian properties. bib. illus.

66. Bureau, Pierre. "Aerial Low-Altitude Photography: A Tool for Field Studies." *APT Bulletin* 22, no.1&2 (1990): pp.85-92.

Inventaire Architectural, 1977-1982, produced 250,000 images of 1,600 Quebec municipalities as tool for typological analysis, compliment to ground level survey. French translation. illus.

67. Burns, John and the staff of HABS/HAER, National Park Service, eds. "Recording Historic Landscapes in Recording Historic Structures." Washington, D.C.: The American Institute of Architects Press, 1989.

Predominantly structures. Includes chapter on the documentation of Meridian Hill Park, Wash., D.C. Detailed plans, sections, photographs. bib. illus.

68. Burton, Nick; Matthews, Russel. "Keeping the Necklace Bright." *Landscape Design* no.185 (Nov.'89): pp.11-13.

Integrated approach for the maintenance and management of the Emerald Necklace, Boston, Mass.; computer management system (MMS) outlined.

69. Butko, Brian A. "Historic Highway Preservation: Not a Dead End Street." *CRM* 16, no.6 (1993): pp.36-39.

   Heritage tourism, economic development, as they relate to highway preservation. Heritage parks, Lincoln Highway, National Road in Pa., discussed. illus.

70. Cairns, Malcolm; Kesler, Gary. "Protecting a Prototype." *Landscape Architecture* 77, no.4 (1987): pp.62-65,100.

   Design guidelines for preservation and rehabilitation of Riverside, designed by Frederick Law Olmsted, Sr. and Calvert Vaux, 1868-69. Focus on planting treatment and management. Applications to other communities. illus.

71. Cameron, Christina. "The Challenges of Historic Corridors." *CRM* 16, no.11 (1993): pp.5-7,60.

   Definitions. Canadian examples: trails, roads, waterways, and railroads. Identification, evaluation and management issues. World Heritage Committee Criteria Application. illus.

72. Campbell, Susan. "A Few Guidelines for the Conservation of Old Kitchen Gardens." *Garden History* 13, no.1 (1985): pp.68-74.

   The treatment of English kitchen garden elements through early twentieth century: heated walls, copings, various storage areas, fruit trees. Equipment. bib. illus.

73. Carr, Ethan. "Landscape Architecture in National Parks: 1916-1942." *CRM* 16, no.4 (1993): pp.7-9.

   Overview of first National Historic Landmark, (NHL) theme study to deal specifically with historic designed landscapes. Components: NHL nomination examples and contextual essay.

74. Cartier, Carolyn L. "Creating Historic Open Space in Melaka." *The Geographical Review* 83, no.4 (1993): pp.359-373.

   Development threats to oldest traditional Chinese burial ground ended. Bukit China, in Malaysia, preserved as open space. Public awareness of historic value and interpretation increases. bib. illus.

75. Cartlidge, Thora, ed. "Cultural Landscape Preservation: The Care and Preservation of Changing Places" *Minnesota Common Ground* 2, no. 1 (1994): 16pp.

   Regional issues include: A Study of the New Federal Reserve Project in Minneapolis, Linda Mack; Commentaries on the Renovation of Nicollet Mall and Minnehaha Park in Minneapolis, Charles Birnbaum; Commentary on Landscape Preservation in the Upper Midwest, Lance Neckar; The Landscape Context in Preserving the LeDuc House in Hastings, Carol Zellie; Campus Preservation at the University of Minn., Frank Edgerton Martin; An Overview of National Park Service Landscape Preservation Projects in the Upper Midwest, Arnold Alanen and Susan Overson; and, Landscape Preservation Strategies for the Lincoln Highway in Nebr., Carol Ahlgren. bib. illus.

76. Carver, Humphrey. "Meadow and Field-Path." *APT Bulletin* 15, no.4 (1983): pp.5-7.

   Transition of Canadian vacation home typology from 'wilderness' settings to 'de-cultivated' agricultural landscapes. How agricultural typology, changing demographics, regional, preservation policy affect land use.

77. Chadbourne, Christopher. "A City of Streets and Squares." *Historic Preservation Forum* 7, no.5 (1993): pp.37-43.

   Re-examination of guidelines for historic preservation developed in 1968 for Savannah, Ga., historic district. illus.

78. Chadwick, George. "Paxton's Design Principles for Birkenhead Park." *Landscape Design* no.188 (Mar.'89): pp.16-17.

   Existing conditions and contemporary interventions for U.K. park noted.

79. Chapman, William. "Hidden Assets." *Historic Preservation Forum* 6, no.4 (1992): pp.19-27.

   Small towns, villages and cities in the Caribbean Islands have developed in ways compatible with 'neo-traditional' planning. Opportunities exist to both preserve local culture and allow for future growth using creative zoning and land use planning. bib.

80.   Clark, H. F. "The Restoration and Reclamation of Gardens."
      Garden History Society Occasional Paper No.1 (1969): pp.3-6.

      Cultural, historical concepts of Nature to be a factor in
      restoration treatment. Cautions against 'too pedantic an
      approach to period accuracy, especially in planting,' in favor
      of consideration of design intent, continuity of time.

81.   Clay, Grady. "Whose Time is This Place? The Emerging
      Science of Garden Preservation." *Landscape Architecture* 66,
      no.3 (1976): pp.217-218.

      Historic perspective and critique of landscape preservation
      practice. The need for research and to plan for the
      landscape's evolution or change. illus.

82.   Cleelend, Teri A. "Route 66 Revisited." *CRM* 16, no.11
      (1993): pp.15-18.

      Arizona highway segment registration. Identification and
      analysis leading to nomination, protection and interpretation.
      bib. illus.

83.   Cliver, E. Blaine. "A New and Dynamic Element of Heritage
      Preservation." *CRM* 16, no.11 (1993): pp.1,8.

      Summary to thematic issue. Transportation corridors link a
      series of features of a common theme or a single linear
      experience of motion through space and time. Need for
      standards.

84.   Clous, Richard. "Historic Residential Landscapes in Georgia:
      The Georgia Living Places Project." *CRM* 14, no.6 (1991):
      pp.4-6,14.

      Two year project consisted of nine county field survey,
      search of State National Register database, and literature
      search. Analysis describes nine distinct regional residential
      landscape forms. Applications: basis for conference, National
      Register Multiple Property documenation form; publication.
      illus.

85. Cobham, Ralph, ed. "Amenity Landscape Management: A Resource Handbook." New York: Van Nostrand, 1990.

     Handbook by partner in U.K. firm that created maintenance management plans for Blenheim; Biltmore, Asheville, N.C., and the Emerald Necklace, Boston, Mass. illus.

86. Cobham, Ralph. "Blenheim: The Art and Management of Landscape Restoration." *Landscape Research* 9, no.2 (1984): pp.4-14.

     Preservation planning recognizing maintenance and visitor pressures at Blenheim, U.K. History of the site from the eighteenth century to the present; treatment, management actions. bib. illus.

87. Coen, Duane; Nassauer, Joan; Tuttle, Ron. *Landscape Architecture in the Rural Landscape.*, American Society of Landscape Architects, Washington, D.C., 1987.

     Preservation planning case studies. Implementation opportunities and constraints. bib. illus.

88. Comp, T. Allan, ed. *Regional Heritage Areas: Approaches to Sustainable Development.*, National Trust for Historic Preservation, Washington, D.C., 1994. 48 pp.

     National overview. Case studies: Southwestern Pennsylvania Heritage Preservation Program, Tennessee Overhill, Southwest Montana, Iowa (Silos and Smokestacks Program), Mississippi Headwaters, and Potomac River Heritage Project. Systems examples: French Heritage Parks, Pennsylvania Heritage Parks. National Coalition background, concept, purpose and principles. Annotated state-by-state national guide. bib. illus.

89. Cook, Edward A. "Urban Landscape Networks: An Ecological Planning Framework." *Landscape Research* 16, no.3 (1991): pp.7-15.

     Implementing concept of an urban landscape network, using Phoenix, Ariz., as example. Assessment of natural, cultural resources; spatial structure (ecological patches, corridors), landscape network types, application at local and regional scales. bib. illus.

90. Cook, Robert. "A Historic Collaboration." *The Public Garden* 8, no.1 (1993): pp.25-27.

    National Park Service North Atlantic Regional Office and Arnold Arboretum, Jamaica Plain, Mass., work together to preserve, interpret historic landscapes. illus.

91. Corbett, Jack; Garcia, Nelly Robles. "Cultural Resources Management in Mexico." *CRM* 17, no.4 (1994): pp.12-15.

    National Institute of Anthropology and History (INAH) founded 1939, has departments for archaeological registry, salvage, underwater archaeology, cultural property restoration, museums and exhibits. Cultural resources management concerned with past, present indigenous population, colonial past, emergence of mestizo society, land tenure. bib. illus.

92. Couch, Sarah M. "The Practice of Avenue Planting in the Seventeenth and Eighteenth Centuries." *Garden History* 20, no.2 (1992): pp.173-200.

    Avenue, a 'designed drive or walk, with regularly planted trees in straight rows,' discussed regarding species type, spacing, installation, and maintenance during the period from 1660-1750. bib. illus.

93. Couch, Sarah M. "Trees in Line for Conservation" *Landscape Design* no.214 (Oct.'92): pp.43-46.

    History of tree allees. Issues of age and maintenance; recommendations for study, analysis, management, replanting. illus.

94. Coupe, Michael; Fairclough, Graham. "Protection for Historic and Natural Landscapes." *Landscape Design* no.201 (June '91): pp.24-30.

    Guide to the different categories of protected status, mandatory and advisory, in the U.K.. illus.

95. Cowley, Jill. "Canyon De Chelly: An Ethnographic Landscape." *CRM* 14, no.6 (1991): pp.10-11.

    Guideline development at National Monument site; field interviews with Navaho indians; visitor experience

implications. Cites National Park Service ethnographic
landscape studies. bib. illus.

96. Cowley, Jill. "The O'Keeffe Landscape: Setting the Stage for
Interpretation." *CRM* 17, no.7 (1994): pp.28-31.

   Interpreting the relationship between the artist, Georgia
O'Keeffe, and the northern N. Mex. landscape. Integrity and
significance findings inform interpretation. Details landscape's
character-defining features through O'Keeffe's personal
descriptions. Treatment alternatives. bib. illus.

97. Crackles, F. E. "Medieval Gardens in Hull: Archeological
Evidence." *Garden History* 14, no.1 (1986): pp.1-5.

   Analysis of plant macrofossils in area presumably used for
gardens. Seed list including sixteenth century fruits, fifteenth
century vegetables. bib. illus.

98. Crankshaw, Ned M. "CARPA: Computer Aided Reverse
Perspective Analysis." *APT Bulletin* 22, no.1&2 (1990):
pp.117-131.

   Computer generated perspective graphics translate
photographs to plan views. Best applied on relatively flat sites
for which historical photographs exist, and where building
from historic period can be measured and grounds are
rectilinear in form. bib. illus.

99. Crawford, Pleasance. "Letters on Landscape." *APT Bulletin*
19, no.2 (1987): pp.61-63.

   Nineteenth century correspondence between Heinrich Adolph
Engelhardt, landscape designer, and John Woodburn
Langmuir, Ontario Dept. of Public Works, regarding designs
for Canadian institutional landscapes. illus.

100. Crawford, Pleasance. "Nineteenth Century Plant Labels."
APT Bulletin 21, no.1 (1989): pp.58-61.

   Historic materials, marking and fastening methods. Research
basis for garden managers and interpreters. bib. illus.

101. Croteau, Todd. "Recording NPS Roads and Bridges." *CRM*
16, no.3 (1993): pp.3-4.

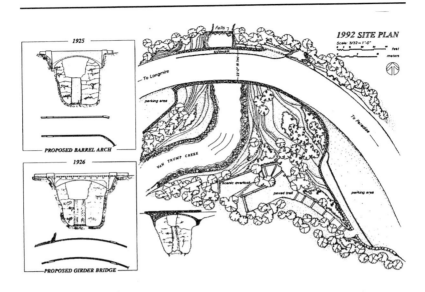

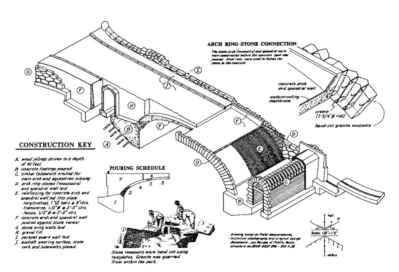

See citation 101: Todd Croteau. "Recording NPS Roads and Bridges." *CRM*, 1993. Plan and elevation of Christine Falls Bridge, built at Mount Rainier National Park in 1928, illustrates the evolution of park service designs (top). Construction detail of Stoneman Bridge, 1932, illustrates the process of bridge building in the parks (bottom).

Fifth year progress report on Historic American Engineering Record (HAER) documentation project producing written narratives, drawings, photographs. National Park Service National Capitol Region completed; western U.S. parks underway. illus.

102. Crusius, Martha; Parkin, Drew. "The Rivers and Trails Program of the National Park Service: Assessing Reso" *Trends* 29, no.2 (1992): pp. 13-17.

    Ten-year program history. The "Riverwork Book" as a tool for resource assessment: documentation and analysis for significance determination, planning, management concensus. Case studies: Bear River Greenway, Wyo.; Delaware and Hudson Canal Heritage Corridor, N.Y.; Wood-Pawcatuck Rivers, R.I.; Horseshoe Trail, Assessment, Pa.; Westfield River Greenway, Mass.; Santa Ana River Trail, Calif.; Northwest Rivers Study, Wash., Oreg., Idaho, Mont.; Lackawanna Valley National Heritage Corridor, Pa. illus.

103. Curk, Iva. "Landscape Protection in Ljubljana, Yugoslavia." *APT Bulletin* 21, no.2 (1989): pp.74-76.

    Historical significance of Ljubljana Moor since Iron Age. Archaeological vernacular landscape features. Contemporary administrative preservation efforts. illus.

104. Currie, Christopher K. "The Archeology of the Flowerpot in England and Wales, circa 1650-1950." *Garden History* 21, no.2 (1993): pp.227-246.

    Description of 'useful' pots, as distinct from 'ornamental' ones. Originally made at local kilns, flower pots were produced on a large scale by mid-nineteenth century. Uses of different shapes analyzed. bib. illus.

105. Currie, Christopher K. "Literary and Archaeological Evidence for Pond Construction Techniques." *Garden History* 18, no.1 (1990): pp.32-46.

    Description of how both fish ponds, decorative ponds and pools were constructed in post-medieval period. Includes archeological and textual evidence. bib. illus.

106. Currie, Christopher K.; Locock, M. "An Evaluation of Archeological Techniques Used at Castle Bromwich Hall, 1989-90." *Garden History* 19, no.1 (1991): pp.77-99.

Summary of techniques available to garden archaeologists. Includes results of experimental techniques. bib. illus.

107. Dalley, Stephanie. "Ancient Mesopotamian Gardens and the Identification of the Hanging Gardens of Babylon Resolved." *Garden History* 21, no.1 (1993): pp.1-13.

Mesopotamian gardens differentiated from later Persian gardens. Explanation, description of 'Hanging Gardens of Babylon,' speculation about the Garden of Eden. illus.

108. Day, Karen E. *Restoring Vine Coverage to Historic Buildings.*, U.S. Department of the Interior. National Park Service Cultural Resources. Preservation Assistance Division., Washington, D.C., 6 pp.

Tech Note case study of nineteenth century trellis restoration project at Fairsted, Frederick Law Olmsted National Historic Site, Brookline, Mass. Historic background and experimental systems. Types: spiraled steel strapping, aircraft cable, modular pipe and combination alternatives. Notes on fabrication, installation, maintenance and findings. Construction details. bib. illus.

109. de Haen, Viktoria. "Knole Park: After the Storm." *Landscape Design* no. 91 (June '90): pp.19-22.

Five hundred year history of Knole Park, Kent, U.K. Impact of 1987 hurricane; restoration efforts, including extant medieval landscape features.

110. DeHart, H. Grant. "The Future of the Preservation Movement." *Historic Preservation Forum* 5, no.5 (1991): pp.6-21.

Issues facing historic preservation movement over the next twenty-five years, including multi-culturalism, land trusts, preserving the recent past, foreign ownership, Geographic Information Systems (GIS). bib.

111. DeHart, H. Grant; Frobuck, Jo Ann. "Preserving Public
     Interests and Property Rights." *Historic Preservation Forum* 7,
     no.4 (1993): pp.36-46.

     Easement program to preserve Civil War battlefields in
     Antietam, Md., resolved conflicts between property rights and
     preservation advocates. illus.

112. Del Tredici, Peter. "The Great Catalpa Craze." *Arnoldia* 46,
     no.2 (1986): pp.2-10.

     History of commercial and ornamental development of the
     deciduous tree. bib. illus.

113. Deloria, Philip S. "The Preservation of Indian Culture."
     Historic Preservation Forum 7, no.1 (1993): pp.42-47.

     Background, issues, opportunities and constraints:
     government funding and involvement balanced with the
     traditional expectations of Native American cultures as they
     relate to historic preservation.

114. Diamont, Rolf. "Continuing Commitment to Landscape
     Preservation." *Courier* 34, no.8 (1989): pp.23-24.

     F. L. Olmsted National Historic Site, Fairsted, Brookline,
     Mass., demonstrates NPS landscape concerns. illus.

115. Diamont, Rolf. "National Heritage Corridors: Redefining the
     Conservation Agenda of the 90's." *The George Wright Forum*
     8, no.2 (1991): pp.13-16.

     Contrast between newly created Blackstone River National
     Heritage Corridor and Great Basin National Park.
     Administrative strategies, rationale and background for
     national heritage corridors in the U.S.

116. Diehl, Janet; Barrett, Thomas S. et al. "The Conservation
     Easement Handbook: Managing Land Conservation and
     Historic Preservation Easement Programs." 4th ed. San
     Francisco, California/Washington, D.C.: Trust for Public
     Land/Land Trust Alliance, (1988): 269 pp.

     Tools to improve land protection efforts. Guidance for
     operating an easement program. Includes: techniques, criteria,
     compliance issues, competing land uses, and ethical

PRELIMINARY PROTECTION PRIORITY CRITERIA

CRITERION	PRIORITY
1. Productive Agricultural Soils	
a. 75-100% "prime" soil	critical
b. 25-74% "prime" soil	high
c. over 25% farmland of statewide importance, with less than 25% "prime" soil	moderate
2. Productive Forest Soils	
a. 51-100% "good" soil	high
b. 25-50% "good" soil	moderate
c. all "fair" productivity soil	moderate
3. Key Tracts	
a. critical to wilderness, primitive or canoe areas	critical
b. small tracts surrounded by Forest Preserve (state land)	high
4. Scenic Vistas	
a. fore and middle ground (0-2 miles)	critical
b. background (2-3 miles)	high
5. Travel Corridors Within Adirondack Park	
a. within resource management zone	high
b. within rural use zone	moderate
6. Significant Natural Resource Areas	
a. major wetlands or important habitats	critical
b. undeveloped shoreline	critical
c. deer wintering areas	moderate
7. Agricultural Districts	moderate
8. Wild, Scenic, and Recreational Rivers System	
a. wild or scenic river corridors	critical
b. recreational river or study river corridors	high
c. National inventory rivers	moderate
9. Adirondack Park Legislatively Designated Open Space	
a. rural use	moderate
b. resource management	moderate

[These criteria are described in detail in a handbook published by the Adirondack Land Trust, Developing a Land Conservation Strategy: A Handbook for Land Trusts. Available from the Adirondack Land Trust or the Land Trust Exchange.]

See citation 116. Janet Diehl, Thomas S. Barrett and others. *The Conservation Easement Handbook: Managing Land Conservation and Historic Preservation Easement Programs.* 4th ed., 1988. Sample criteria for land protection assessments for a number of organizations are included.

resposibilities. Appendices: Model easement, IRS requirement checklist and national contacts. illus.

117. Dimbleby, G. W. "Pollen as Botanical Evidence of the Past." *Landscape Architecture* 66, no.3 (1976): pp.219-223.

Pollen and charcoal analysis in Greek garden archaeology projects at Pompeii, Hercules, Plybius, Europa, and Calci. Determination of species and distribution of plant materials. illus.

118. Doherty, Jonathan. "Conserving Historic Landscapes Beyond Park Boundaries." *Courier* 34, no.8 (1989): pp.31-33.

National Park Service need to identify and set objectives for adjacent lands. Management often controversial, especially regarding privately owned land. George Washington Birthplace National Monument, Tidewater, Va., discussed. illus.

119. Dolinsky, Paul D. "HABS: 54 Years of Documenting Historic Landscapes." *Landscape Architecture* 77, no.4 (1987): pp.86-89.

History of National Park Service cultural landscape preservation program. Examples of Historic American Buildings Survey (HABS) documentation projects: 'The Vale,' Waltham, Mass.,, Captain Thomas Bennett House 'Sunken Garden,' Fairhaven, Mass., Recent summer landscape documentation, example: Meridian Hill Park, Washington, D.C. (1985). illus.

120. Dolinsky, Paul D. "Landscape Recording: Expanding the Tradition." *CRM* 9, no.3 (1986): pp.16-17.

Recent landscape documentation projects at the Historic American Buildings Survey (HABS). illus.

121. Donahue, John. "Managing Orchards, A Difficult Resource." *CRM* 8, no.5 (1985): pp.3,5,13.

Management plan for the John Muir National Historic Site, Martinez, Calif. illus.

122. Donaldson, Sue. "Monumental and Other Purposes." *APT Bulletin* 15, no.4 (1983): pp.23-26.

    Contemporary design and uses of monuments questioned, based upon generational public perceptions of history, commemoration, contemplation, recreation. bib.

123. Drayman-Weisser, Terry. "Dialogue/89: The Conservation of Bronze Sculpture in the Outdoor Environment: A Dialogue Among Conservators, Curators, Environmental Scientists, and Corrosion Engineers." Houston, Texas: NACE (National Association of Corrosion Engineers), 1992, 390 pp.

125. Dyer, Delce; Bass, Quentin. "Southern Appalachian National Forests: Interpretive Planning for Rural Historic Landscapes." *CRM* 17, no.7 (1994): pp.23-27.

    USDA Forest Service management of over 400 million acres in six forests, including many Civilian Conservation Corps (CCC) resources. Cherokee National Forest, Tenn.,measuring 630,000 acres case study. Management decisions informed by documentation and evaluation of cultural resources (e.g. native American sites, upland grazing, farmsteads, firetowers). bib. illus.

126. Ebert, James I.; Gutierrez, Alberto A. "Relationships Between Landscapes and Archeological Sites in Shenandoah National Park: A Remote Sensing Approach." *APT Bulletin* 11, no.4 (1979): pp.69-87.

    Aerial color infrared photographic study of two densely vegetated sites. Computerized data records slope, aspect, ground cover, proximity to geographic fault zones, and helps predict archaeological cultural resource materials. bib. illus.

127. Edwards, Mark R. "Protecting the Public Landscape of a National Historic Landmark." *Historic Preservation Forum* 5, no.4 (1991): pp.16-28.

    St. Mary's Townlands Study Committee, a public/private Maryland group, developed a comprehensive planning initiative to better protect Historic St. Mary's City (HSMC), a publicly administered National Historic Landmark. illus.

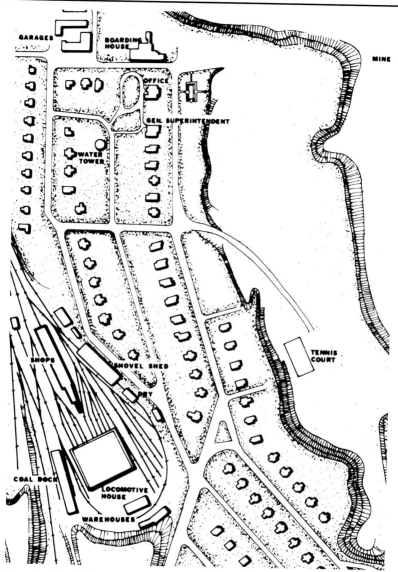

See citation 126. James I. Ebert and Alberto A Gutierrez. "Relationships Between Landscapes and Archeological Sites in Shenandoah National Park: A Remote Sensing Approach." *APT Bulletin*, 1979. By using various cartographic and pictorial sources it was possible to recreate the plans for locations such as Mahoninh, Minn.

128. Edwards, Paul. "Wroxton Abbey: Research for Restoration Proposals." *Landscape Research* 4, no.3 (1979): pp.18-19.

Fairleigh Dickinson University, N.J., purchased Wroxton Abbey, near Banbury, U.K., and opened the restored campus in 1965. Excerpts from historic grounds report forming basis of grant application to Historic Buildings Council. bib. illus.

129. Einset, John W. "Replacing the Understory Plantings of Central Park." *Arnoldia* 45, no.2 (1985): pp.19-27.illus.

130. Elliot, Brent. "The Landscape of the English Cemetery" *Landscape Design* no. 184 (Oct.'89): pp.13-14.

Nineteenth century to present discussion, includes contemporary management and maintenance. bib.

131. Ellwand, Nancy. "Motherwell Homestead: Restoration of a Landscape." *APT Bulletin* 15, no.4 (1983): pp.66-71.

Saskatchewan homesite of William Richard Motherwell (1860-1943), Western Canadian agrarian movement leader, restored by Parks Canada, including shelter belts, gardens, site furnishings. Maintenance guidelines implemented. Management plan approved, 1981. bib. illus.

132. Ellwood, Brooks B. "Electrical Resistivity Surveys in Two Historical Cemeteries in Northeast Texas: A Method for Delineating Unidentified Burial Shafts." *Historical Archaeology* 24, no.3 (1990): pp.91-98.

Non-destructive soils study used to augment archival records; aid in cemetery relocation. bib. illus.

133. Everson, Paul. "The Gardens of Campden House, Chipping Campden, Gloucester." *Garden History* 17, no.2 (1989): pp.109-121.

Analysis of earthworks remaining from Jacobean house, including terraces, canals, water parterre, orchard, fishpond. Influence of continental designs and contemporary English gardens. bib. illus.

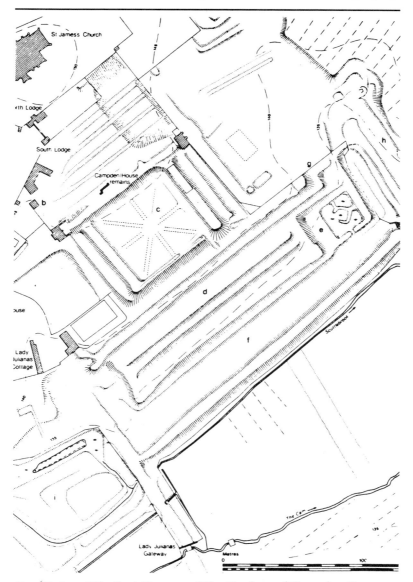

See citation 133: Paul Everson. "The Gardens of Campden House, Chipping Campden, Gloucester." *Garden History*, 1989. Drawing of the earthwork survey of formal garden remains at Campden House.

134. Fairbanks, Charles H. "The Plantation Archaeology of the Southeastern Coast." *Historical Archaeology* 18, no.1 (1984): pp.1-14.

    Impact of recent slave settlement archaeological investigation on historical archaeology, and cultural resources managment. Southeastern U.S. coastal sites in Ga., and S.C., principal field work study areas. bib.

135. Fairclough, Graham. "New Landscapes of Conservation." *Conservation Bulletin* 22, (1994): pp.16-17.

    Cooperation between English Heritage, English Nature and the Countryside Commission in the U.K. Summary of partnership projects 1991-93. Pilot projects include: experimentation with assessment methodologies; review of historic landscape work in surveys and environmental impact statements; raising public awareness; clarifying concepts, terminology and framework. illus.

136. Fardin, Linda DiCaire. "Assessing the Cultural Value of Historic Parks and Gardens." *APT Bulletin* 24, no.3&4 (1992): pp.14-24.

    Canadian criteria for assessing cultural value of parks and gardens adapted from Canadian Federal Heritage Buildings Review, and English Heritage system. Aesthetic, historic features quantified. bib. illus.

137. Fardin, Linda DiCaire. "Assessment Strategies for Canada's Historic Sites." *CRM* 16, no.4 (1993): pp.14-16.

    Quantitative evaluation method for landscapes. Rideau Hall National Historic Site case study. bib. illus.

138. Favretti, Rudy J.; Favretti, Joy Putnam. "Landscapes and Gardens for Historic Buildings." Nashville, Tenn.: American Association for State and Local History, 1978.

    Focus on "period" gardens. Includes a short history of design, and,research, documentation and maintenance techniques. Source list of plants grouped by time period. bib., annotated. illus.

139. Fedelchak, Marilyn. "A Thirst for History: An Assessment of the Compatibility of the Federal Rural-Development Programs and Historic Preservation." *Historic Preservation Forum* 5, no.6 (1991): pp.17-39.

     Assessment of federal rural development programs and compatibility with local, state, federal historic preservation programs and projects in rural areas.

140. Feierabend, Carey. "Managing Change in a Cultural Landscape." *CRM* 12, no.2 (1989): pp.7-8.

     Cultural Landscape Report findings for Boxley Valley Rural Historic District, Ozark Mountains, Ark. Balancing natural and cultural issues. Visual compatibility guidelines for new construction. illus.

141. Feierabend, Carey. "The Presidio of San Francisco's Cultural Landscape." *CRM* 14, no.6 (1991): pp.12-14.

     Interdisciplinary analysis of 1,400 acre landscape with 200 years of military history. Project summary: inventory, research (including 1776-1990 chronology), documentation, condition assessment, definition of character-defining features. illus.

142. Firth, Ian J. W. "Biotic Resources in Historic Landscapes." *Courier* 34, no.8 (1989): pp.14-15.

     Need to recognize historical significance; currently not recognized in National Register criteria. Example: Historic Orchards Survey. illus.

143. Firth, Ian J. W. "For Beauty or Business: Farmland Preservation on Villa, Estate, and Plantation." *Landscape Architecture* 73, no.1 (1983): pp.62-68.

     Balancing preservation and economic interests at three agricultural landscapes: a Tuscan villa farm, Italy; an eighteenth century estate, Yorkshire, U.K.; and a tidewater plantation, Ga. illus.

144. Fitch, James Marston. "Preservation Requires Tact, Modesty and Honesty Among Designers." *Landscape Architecture* 66, no.3 (1976): pp.276-280.

Historic perspective of historic preservation philosophy as applied to landscapes. illus.

145. Fly, Everett L.; Fly, La Barbara Wigfall. "Ethnic Landscapes Come to Light." *Landscape Architecture* 77, no.4 (1987): pp.34-39.

    Absence of multicultural representation in rural landscape documentation projects. Comprehensive inventory approach; use of census data, oral history, physical evidence. Multi-disciplinary approaches. Analysis of findings. Examples from New England, Pacific coast, Alaska. illus.

146. Ford, Steve; Bowden, Mark; Gaffney, Vince; Mees, Geoff. "Dating Ancient Field Systems on the Berkshire Downs in England." *Expedition (The University Museum Magazine of Archaeology and Anthropology, University of Pennsylvania)* 32, no.2 (1990): pp.44-51.

    Determination of Roman origins based upon analysis of hill forts, linear ditches, lynchets, with aerial photography, and artifacts such as pottery sherds, flint, snail shells, with trench excavation. bib. illus.

147. Fortin, Lucie. "The Evolution and Persistence of Three Land Division Systems in the Green Bay Region of Wisconsin." *Landscape Journal* 7, no.1 (1988): pp.47-59.

    Compares French long-lots, the American Public Land Survey, and the Williams Grant (a local application), using computerized Geographic Information System (GIS). bib. illus.

148. Fox, Kathleen M.; Southerland, Robert J.; Weisner, Elizabeth. "Rehabilitating State House Grounds: Building Consensus." *Landscape Architecture* 78, no.1 (1988): pp.64-67.

    The treatment of the Ky. capitol landscape, originally designed by the Olmsted Brothers in 1908. illus.

149. Franklin, Colin. "Why Acquire Buffer Land?" *The Public Garden* 3, no.2 (1988): pp.12-15.

Acquisition and management of landscape buffers to ensure visual, spatial, ecological integrity of historic properties. illus.

150. Fricker, Jonathan. "Transportation History and the Louisiana Comprehensive Plan." *CRM* 16, no.11 (1993): pp.24-25,40.

Historic overview of the steamboat, railroad and early automobile eras. Efforts to preserve historic properties in their corridor context. illus.

151. Friedman, Renee. "Of Trees and Teacups: The Landscape as Artifact." *CRM* 17, no.7 (1994): pp.5-6,9.

Reprint of article from July-August 1988 "History News." Landscape interpretation philosophy for stewards. Considers interpretation as communication of change over time; need to link landscape and houses and collections for unified interpretation; importance of vegetation as indicator of relationship of people and nature. bib. illus.

152. Fry, Bruce W. "My Life is in Ruins: The Limitations of Stabilization as a Presentation Technique." *CRM* 15, no.8 (1992): pp.7-8.

Presentation, interpretation at sites of stabilized masonry ruins. illus.

153. Gagliardi, Neil; Morris, Stephen. "Local Historic Preservation Plans: A Selected Annotated Bibliography." Washington, D.C.: Branch of Preservation Planning, Interagency Resources Division, National Park Service, U.S. Department of the Interior, 1993.

Results of national survey of 1,800 communities. Emphasis on regional diversity, scale variety, scope and linking preservation with community concerns. Includes comprehensive and area preservation plans. Sample plans and charts. illus.

154. Gaines, David; Gomez, Art. "Perspectives on Route 66." *CRM* 16, no.11 (1993): pp.21-23.

Historical values of sixty-six year old, 2,400 mile roadway from Chicago, Ill., to Los Angeles, Calif. Commemoration,

preservation, interpretation; management and partnership
opportunities. bib. illus.

155. Garate, Donald T. "The Juan Bautista de Anza National
Historic Trail." *CRM* 16, no.11 (1993): pp. 36-38.

Interpretation of 1,800 mile trail of the 1775-76 Anza
Expedition in Calif., and Mexico. History, description of
existing conditions, interpretive goals include appreciation of
cultural diversity. illus.

156. Giamberdine, Richard V.; Beal, Lawrence E.; Dunbar, Keith
B.; Johnson, Ronald W. "Upper Delaware National Scenic
and Recreational River: A Process to Protect a Rural
Landscape." *The George Wright Forum* 3, no.1 (1983):
pp.42-49.

National Park Service-coordinated management plan for river
designated part of Wild and Scenic River System in 1978,
allowing for minimal federal land acquisition.
Multi-disciplinary approach. illus.

157. Gibson, Dierdre; Rivinus, Willis M.; Sachse, C. Allen;
Mineo, Isadore C. "The Delaware and Lehigh Canal National
Heritage Corridor: Community-Based Partnerships and their
Impacts." *Trends* 29, no.2 (1992): pp.23-30.

Preservation of a 150-mile canal corridor and its setting in
eastern Pa., including related industry, historic towns and
agricultural lands. Description of partnership organizations
and commissions, preservation planning and benefits. illus.

158. Giebner, Robert C. "Probing the Issues of Town/Gown
Conflict." *Historic Preservation Forum* 6, no.6 (1992): pp.
18-32.

Current issues and recommended actions between campuses
and their neighborhood settings. Institutions, municipalities
and residents working together. Historic perspective.

159. Gilbert, Cathy. "Another Look: Landscape Perspectives."
CRM 11, no.3 (1988): pp.4-5.

Identification of significant features at Fort Spokane and
interpretation to the public. illus.

160. Gilbert, Cathy. "Cultural Landscapes and the New Technologies." *Public Historian* 13, no.3 (1991): pp. 109-112.

   Discussion of strengths, weaknesses of traditional and emerging landscape documentation technologies and their ability to inform management decisions about cultural landscapes.

161. Gilbert, Cathy. "NPS Pacific Northwest Region Cultural Landscape Inventory." *CRM* 14, no.6 (1991): pp. 15-17.

   Summary of phase one, comprehensive program and systematic process to identify, document, evaluate cultural landscapes in each park. Olympic National Park, Wash., example. illus.

162. Gilbert, Cathy. "The Tao House Courtyard: Exposing a Playwright's Garden." *CRM* 10, no.6 (1987): pp.1, 3-6.

   The restoration treatment for a walled garden at National Park site in Danville, Calif. illus.

163. Gilbert, Cathy. "Tools of the Trade: Methodologies in Landscape Preservation." *The George Wright Forum* 8, no.2 (1991): pp.2-12.

   Definitions, examples of inventory, documentation, analysis, evaluation, treatment. Need to distinguish between nostalgia and preservation; link practice with scholarship. bib. illus.

164. Gittings, Kirk. *Introduction to Photographing Historic Properties.*, National Trust for Historic Preservation, Washington, D.C., 1992. 16 pp.

   Tools, techniques and processes. Artistic and documentary methodologies. Considerations: on-site, selecting film, processing, printing and storage. Focus on structures. Photography standards from the Historic American Buildings Survey (HABS) and the National Register. bib. illus.

165. Gleason, Kathryn Louise. "The Garden Portico of Pompey the Great." *Expedition (The University Museum Magazine of Archaeology and Anthropology, University of Pennsylvania)* 32, no.2 (1990): pp.4-13.

Third century A.D. marble plan of Rome, extant literary texts, physical remains, used to locate public parks and promenades from Republican and Imperial periods. bib. illus.

166. Gleason, Kathryn Louise. "A Garden Excavation in the Oasis Palace of Herod the Great at Jerico." *Landscape Journal* 12, no.2 (1991): pp. 156-167.

Excavation of the Garden at the Herodian complex, using stratigraphy and environmental and artifactual data. Plan and perspective 'reconstruction' drawings generated based on findings. illus.

167. Glime, Nancy. "Walking Through History." *Landscape Architect* 10, no.4 (1994): pp.22-23.

Landscape architects and artists collaborate on sculpture and in-laid paving details depicting and interpreting community history. National examples. illus.

168. Goeldner, Paul K. ,. Dr. "Plant Life at Historic Properties." *APT Bulletin* 16, no.3&4 (1984): pp.67-69.

Vegetative threats to historic structures, cemeteries, industrial ruins, historic battlefields. Eighteen sites surveyed by National Park Service Capital Region in 1982. bib. illus.

169. Goetcheus, Cari. "Visual Assessment Strategies: Crossing the Line From Landscape Architecture to Historic Preservation." *Georgia Landscape* (1994): p.15.

Influence of 1960s developments in visual analysis on landscape preservation since the 1970s--the need to further explore this relationship.

170. Goodchild, Peter. "Conservation of Gardens and Parks of Historic Interest in the United Kingdom: A Note." *APT Bulletin* 11, no.4 (1979): pp.101-107.

Design strategy for comprehensive survey to identify, describe, and illustrate historic gardens and parks. Overview of trial survey, sample survey forms.

171. Goodchild, Peter. "The Conservation of Parks and Gardens in the United Kingdom." *Landscape Research* 9, no.2 (1984): pp.1-3.

    Editorial on the value of park and gardens as part of cultural heritage of U.K.. Lists issues which impinge on conservation.

172. Goodman, John A. "Turf Management at Drayton Hall." *APT Bulletin* 11, no.4 (1979): pp.26-30.

    Turf grass management experiment at National Trust site in Charleston, S.C. History of lawn care at the property. Considerations for type of mower, grass height, and staff implications to achieve an historically appropriate, maintainable lawn. bib. illus.

173. Goto, Junko; Alanen, Arnold R. "The Conservation of Historic and Cultural Resources in Rural Japan." *Landscape Journal* 6, no.1 (1987): pp.42-61.

    Five case studies from Japan: Tsumago, Shirakawa, Ohuchi, Asuke, and Uchiko. bib. illus.

174. Goulty, Sheena Mackellar. "Heritage Gardens: Care, Conservation and Management." London and New York: Routledge, 1993. 176 pp.

    Eleven international historic garden case studies. Chapters on conservation, maintenance, management. Contemporary photographs depict specific strategies. illus.

175. Greer, Nora Richter; Russell, James S. "Preservation's Vast New Horizons." *Architectural Record* (1994): pp.24-27.

    Industrial Heritage Corridors represent a shift in preservation planning. Discussion of rationale; examples since 1984 inception; activities in southwestern Pa., river corridor, site of steel, coal, transportation industry. illus.

176. Gribben, Thomas; Tulloch, Judith. "Ardgowan--The Restoration of an Island Garden." *APT Bulletin* 18, no.1&2 (1986): pp.99-105.

    Preservation of four acre remnant property of William Henry Pope, mid-nineteenth century Colonial Secretary for Prince

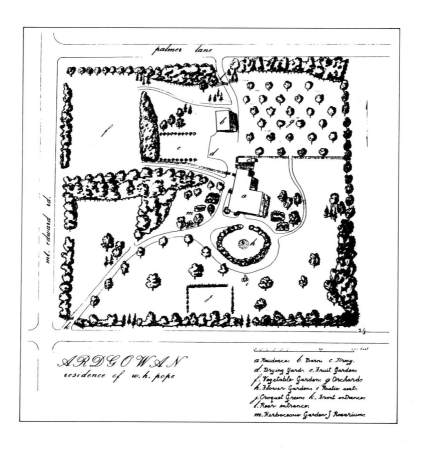

ARDGOWAN
residence of w. h. pope

a. Residence. b. Barn. c. Privy.
d. Drying Yard. e. Fruit Garden.
f. Vegetable Garden. g. Orchard.
h. Flower Garden. i. Rustic seat.
j. Croquet Green. k. Front entrance.
l. Rear entrance.
m. Herbaceous Garden. f. Rosarium.

See citation 176: Thomas Gribben and Judith Tulloch.
"Ardgowan--The Restoration of an Island Garden." *APT Bulletin*,
1986. Historic aerial view rendering of the Pope residence.

44

Edward Island, Canada. Research informing treatment, interpretation. Archival, archaeological investigation. Soil core sample testing with analysis of phosphate and ph. Seed analysis. bib. illus.

177. Groth, Paul, ed. "Vision, Culture and Landscape." Berkeley, California: Department of Landscape Architecture, University of California, Berkeley, 1990.

Dividing Lines and Meeting Ground in Cultural Landscape Interpretation, a preface by Paul Groth. Papers include: Bigger Than a Breadbox, Smaller Than the Cosmos: Twenty Questions About the Landscape Experience, Robert Riley; The Integrity of the Landscape Movement, Jay Appleton; The Future of the Vernacular Landscape, J.B. Jackson; Social Landscapes of a Streetcar Suburb: 1889-1930 Jim Borchert; The Bureau of Indian Affairs Landscape within Santa Clara Pueblo, Rina Swentzell; The Potential of Ethnic Places for Urban Landscape History, Dolores Hayden; Cityscape of Old Chinatowns in North America, David Chuenyan Lai; Hallowed Ground and Rituals of Remembrance: Union Regimental Monuments at Gettysburg, Reuben M. Rainey; The Visual Landscape Resource Idea, R. Burton Litton, Jr.; Community Control versus the Elitist Landscape, Richard C. Smardon; Whose Vision? Whose Meanings? Whose Values? Pluralism and Objectivity in Landscape Analysis, Allen Carlson; The Politics of Vision, Anthony King; The Landscape and the Archives: Texts for the Analysis of the Built Environment, Deryck W. Holdsworth; Where the One-Eyed Man is King: The Epistemological Premises of Visual Analysis, Catherine Howett; Spectacle and Society: Landscape as Theater in Pre-Modern and Post-Modern Cities, Denis Cosgrove. bib. illus.

178. *Guidelines for the Treatment of Historic Landscapes (Draft).*, U.S. Department of the Interior. National Park Service Preservation Assistance Division. Technical Preservation Services Branch., Washington, D.C., 1990, 107 pp.

In-depth guidance for landscapes. Draft document parallels the Guidelines for Rehabilitating Historic Buildings with "recommeded" and "not Recommended" approach. Placement of treatment in preservation planning context and description of historic landscape features. Definitions. bib.

179. Gulliford, Andrew. "Tribal Preservation: An Overview of Cultural Management." *Historic Preservation Forum* 6, no.6 (1992): pp.33-43.

Historic preservation in the case of tribal preservation involves values, cultural heritage, landscape preservation and repatriation of sacred relics and burial remains. bib. illus.

180. Gulliver, Richard Dr. "Reconstructing A Historic Landscape" *Landscape Design* no.181 (June '89): pp.38-41.

Efforts to study, interpret, reconstruct Wharram Percy: DMV ('Deserted Medieval Village'), North Yorkshire, U.K. Includes survey, historical research, reconstruction, maintenance. illus.

181. Hackett, Brian. "Landscape Conservation." Chichester: Packard Publishing Ltd., 1980. 111 pp.

Identification of historic landscape types. Planning and management tools. bib. illus.

182. Hardesty, Donald L. "Evaluating Site Significance in Historical Mining Districts." *Historical Archaeology* 24, no.2 (1990): pp.42-51.

Revitalization of mining in western U.S. leads to growth of archaeological research. Author proposes significance evaluation matrix as quantitative aid in determining mining site inclusion in National Register of Historic Places. bib. illus.

183. Harris, Donna Ann. "Philadelphia's Preservation Initiative." *Historic Preservation Forum* 6, no.5 (1992): pp.10-19.

Impact of Philadelphia's 1991 Transfer of Development Rights (TDR) program on future preservation project work. Rehabilitation and management. Case studies in land conservation: New Jersey Pinelands; Montgomery County, Md.; San Francisco, Calif.; New York City, N.Y.. bib.

184. Harris, Ted and Cathy. "Waterscapes Rediscovered." *Landscape Design* no.182 (July/Aug.'89): pp.39-41.

New methods of dredging water bodies without damage to vegetation; equipment, recycling materials discussed.

185. Hart, John. "Farming on the Edge: Saving Family Farms in Marin County, California." Berkeley and Los Angelos, California: University of California Press, 1991. 174 pp.

   Essays include: Waiting for the End; Back from the Edge; Crisis and Alliance; Something More Permanent; The Land in Trust; Marin the Model; A Grassland History; What Marin County Did (and Didn't Do). illus.

186. Harvey, Mary MacKay. "Gardens of Shelburne, Nova Scotia." *APT Bulletin* 7, no.2 (1975): pp. 32-72.

   Research for treatment of the Ross-Thomson House. Contextual social analysis of the region, 1785-1820. Plant list assembled consulting diaries, letters, historic horticultural literature, illustrative material, and a botanist. Common name plant list. bib. illus.

187. Harvey, Robert R. "An Approach to Developing a Documented and Quantified Plant List." *APT Bulletin* 21, no.2 (1989): pp.51-57.

   Quantitative analysis used to determine plant selection accuracy for Lincoln Home National Historic District, Springfield, Ill. Circa 1860 local, out-of-state nursery catalogues analyzed to determine probability of availability, particularly for exotic (introduced) plant species. bib. illus.

188. Harvey, Robert R. "A Computer Generated Keyword Index to the Selection of Plant Material for Plumb Grove, Iowa." *APT Bulletin* 11, no.4 (1979): pp.31-48.

   Treatment for nineteenth century orchard at the Lucas House farmstead. Analysis of 1854 city map of Plumb Grove, Iowa for orchard restoration. Historic plum tree data numbered. Variety names, bibliographic sources entered, annotated. Notes on herbarium collections today. bib. illus.

189. Harvey, Robert R. "Fieldwork Techniques as an Aid in Reading the Cultural Landscape." *APT Bulletin* 22, no.1&2 (1990): pp.132-141.

On-site and archival techniques establish landscape context, period of significance, origins, impacts and change, combined with soil and solar orientation analysis. Photographic methods. U.S. and U.K. examples. bib. illus.

190. Haskell, David A. "Protecting Park Resources within a Developing Landscape." *The George Wright Forum* 8, no.1 (1991): pp.2-6.

Metropolitan Washington, D.C. expansion, suburbanization puts pressure on Shenandoah National Park, whose Related Lands Initiative suggests management strategies, and creates Geographic Information Systems (GIS) database. bib. illus.

191. Heeb, Mark. "Farmland Preservation: A Model in Chester County, PA." *Georgia Landscape* (1994): p.12.

Overview of cooperative planning tool using existing state conservation legislation, a county open space bill and private conservation initiatives to preserve agricultural and rural community character.

192. Henry, Susan L. "Protecting Archeological Sites on Private Lands." Washington, D.C.: National Park Service, Preservation Planning Branch, Interagency Resources Division, 1993.

Archaeological values, regulatory, and non-regulatory strategies. Annotated appendices: protection strategies; the assessment process; seeking expertise; developer liasion; financial assistance; federal laws. bib. illus.

193. Heritage Conservation and Recreation Service, U.S. Department of the Interior. "New Directions in Rural Preservation." Washington, D.C.: Heritage Conservation and Recreation Service, U.S. Department of the Interior, 1980. 114 pp. bib. illus.

194. Herr, Philip B. "The Case of the Northeastern Village." *Historic Preservation Forum* 6, no.5 (1992): pp.20-28.bib. illus. National Trust Northeast Regional Office Project PREPARE, begun in 1989, in which planners and

See citation 192: Susan L Henry. *Protecting Archeological Sites on Private Lands*. National Park Service, Preservation Planning Branch, Interagency Resources Division, 1993. Aerial View of Cliff Palace, a ca. 1200 A.D. Anasazi cliff dwelling in Mesa Verde National Park, Colo.

preservationists preserve small towns, community character. Roles for advocates. Summary, strategies, publications.

195. Herr, Philip B. "Saving Place: A Guide and Report Card for Protecting Community Character." Boston, Massachusetts: National Trust for Historic Preservation, 1991. 50 pp.

Project of the Northeast Regional Office. Introduction to broad community preservation and management strategies. Check list for residents to evaluate their communities. Glossary, list of organizations. bib., annotated. illus.

196. Hill, John W.; Mahan, Catherine; Johns, Ferdinand. "The Changing View from Mount Vernon." *Landscape Architecture* 71, no.1 (1981): pp.73-76.

Historic perspective of preservation efforts from the 1950s to 1970s at Fairfax County, Va., National Historic Landmark. Public and private efforts. National Colonial Farm case study. illus.

197. "Historical Research in the National Park Service." *CRM* 17, no.5 (1994): pp.1-12.

1993-1994 project list by Park Service region includes principal investigator(s), project title, status, publications available.

198. Holliday, Gary. "Ancient And Modern." *Landscape Design* no. 185 (Nov.'89): pp.16-17.

Problems in Side, Tukish Mediterranean coastal town, in reconciling tourism with the need to protect ancient ruins. illus.

199. Holtz Kay, Jane. "Parkmakers Lookout." *Landscape Architecture* 76, no.6 (1986): pp.144,130.

Changing attitudes in open space advocacy and opportunities in historic landscape preservation projects. National overview. illus.

200. Homewood, Andy. "Working with the Past." *Landscape Design* no.221 (June '93): pp.33-34.

New academic degree program at Sheffield University, U.K., combines landscape architecture and archaeology.

201. Hornbeck, Peter L. "The Garden as Fine Art: Its Maintenance and Preservation. In "Beatrix Jones Farrand: Fifty Years of American Landscape Architecture." Washington, D.C.: Dumbarton Oaks, 1982. pp. 127-137.

     Establishes the importance of maintenance techniques to the designer and the need for current techniques to respond to design intent. Uses Farrand's 'Plant Book for Dumbarton Oaks' as example. bib. illus.

202. Hough, Michael. "The Urban Landscape: The Hidden Frontier." *APT Bulletin* 15, no.4 (1983): pp.9-14.bib.

203. Howett, Catherine. "Interpreting a Painful Past: Birmingham's Kelly Ingram Park." *CRM* 17, no.7 (1994): pp.38-40.

     Rehabilitation of historic Ala. square, post-1963 civil rights rally site. Incorporation of public art into the thematic structure of design. Implications of recent social unrest on site interpretation. bib. illus.

204. Howett, Catherine. "Second Thoughts." *Landscape Architecture* 77, no.4 (1987): pp.52-55.

     Preservation beyond structures. Need for theoretical bases, written history, context, to make informed decisions. Opposition to fake history, 'period' treatments.

205. Hughes, Mary V. "Cultural Landscape Program Development in the NPS Midwest Regional Office." *CRM* 14, no.6 (1991): pp.20-21,26.

     Responsiblilities of newly created cultural landscape position over thirty-three parks. History of efforts since 1970s; initiation of Cultural Landscape Inventory; training, management, treatment.

206. Hume, Aubrey Noel. "Historical Archeology in Garden Restoration." *Landscape Architecture* 66, no.3 (1979): pp.259-264.

Research tools to understand a historic garden's features and spatial organization. illus.

207. Hume, Cyril D. "The Point Ellice House Garden: Recovery and Restoration." *APT Bulletin* 21, no.2 (1989): pp.28-42.

Victoria, British Columbia site occupied by O'Reilly family, 1868-1975. Thorough extant archival documentation of house and garden used in determining garden restoration. Discussion of vegetation renewal. Site interpretation includes restoration process, family, broader social historical context. bib. illus.

208. Humphrey, David T. "The Evolving Landscape at Cuyahoga Valley National Recreation Area." *CRM* 14, no.6 (1991): pp.18-19.

1974 enabling legislation, park history, recognition of historic and pre-historic resource value(s). 1988 Cultural Landscape Report primary themes: pre-history, settlement, transportation, agriculture, industry and recreation. Management, maintenance, implementation. illus.

209. Hunt, John Dixon; Wolschke-Bulmahn, Joachim, eds. "The Vernacular Garden." Washington, D.C.: Dumbarton Oaks, Trustees for Harvard University, 1993. 165 pp.

Proceedings from Dumbarton Oaks Symposium. Papers: The Past and Present of the Vernacular Garden, John B. Jackson; The Hortillonages: Reflections on a Vanishing Gardiners' Culture, Michel Conan; Private Urban Gardening in England, 1700-1830: On the Art of Sinking, Todd Longstaffe-Gowan; The Gardens of African-Americans in the Rural South, Richard Westmacott; The Making of Vernacular Taste: The Case of "Sunset" and "Southern Living," Peirce Lewis; The Garden Landscape: A Popular Aesthetic, Bernard Lassus. Index. bib. illus.

210. Hynd, Neil R.; Ewart, Gordon. "Aberdour Castle Gardens." *Garden History* 11, no.2 (1983): pp.93-111.

Description of archaeological work at fourteenth century Aberdour Castle near Edinburgh, Scotland, trying to establish validity of early plans and to date remains. Appended 1691 plant list. bib. illus.

211. ICOMOS International Symposium: Old Cultures in New
Worlds., 10-15 October 1987. Washington, D.C.: US
ICOMOS, 1987. 1076 pp.

Includes six landscape-related papers: 'The Preservation of
the Historic City Centre of Galle, Sri Lanka,' Ashley Devos
(pp.23-30); Thomas Jefferson's University of
Virginia-Restoration of the Academical Village, James Murray
Howard (pp.64-71); The Re-evaluating of the Site of the
Former Cistercian Abbey of Herkenrode by Integrating into it
a New Monastery for the Regular Canonesses of the Holy
Sepulchre, Lucas van Herck (pp.227-234); The Conservation
of Buildings and Gardens of the Dessau-Worlitz Reformatory
Work, Helmut Stelzer (pp.784-791); European Folk
Architecture in Wisconsin: The Transfer of Old World
Building Traditions to a New World Setting, William A.
Tishler (pp. 792-799); Land Use Planning and the
Conservation and Management of World Heritage Sites of
Kilwa Kisiwani and Songo Mnara, Tanzania, Amini A. Mturi
(pp.977-984). illus.

212. International Perspectives on Cultural Parks: Proceedings of
the First World Conference., Mesa Verde National Park,
Colorado, 16-21 September 1984. Washington, D.C.: U.S.
National Park Service in association with the Colorado
Historical Society, 1989. 408 pp.
Seventy-one papers by archaeologists, anthropologists,
historians, architects, curators, lawyers, politicians,
economists, government officials, planners, political scientists,
representatives of private foundations and academia,
Indigenous cultures from U.S., Panama, and Australia. illus.

213. International Symposium on the Conservation of Urban
Squares and Parks., Montreal, Canada, 12-15 May 1993.
Quebec: Association Des Architectes, 391 pp.

Ninety-three papers from Canada, the U.S., U.K., Denmark,
New-Zealand, Australia, Spain, Turkey, France, Switzerland,
Mexico, Malaysia, Italy and Singapore explore the history of
urban parks and squares, historical and archaeological research
methodologies, site inventories, recording, documentation,
analysis, treatment, management, maintenance and ecology.

214. Jackson, John Brinkerhoff. "Discovering the Vernacular Landscape." New Haven, Connecticut: Yale University Press, 1984. 165 pp.

   A cultural geographer's perspective on interpreting the vernacular landscape. Definitions. Reading landscape types and features including natural spaces, roads, forests, parks and habitats. bib. illus.

215. Jacques, David. "'The Chief Ornament' of Gray's Inn: The Walks from Bacon to Brown." *Garden History* 17, no.1 (1989): pp.41-65.

   Methodological description of two hundred year history of work on the site, including plans, expense records, and plant lists. bib. illus.

216. Jacques, David. "Landscape Interpretation in the United Kingdom: A Historical Perspective and Outlook." *CRM* 17, no.7 (1994): pp.7-9.

   Origin of discipline with the world's first guidebook, 1744, for the gardens at Stowe. Eighteenth and nineteenth century examples. Contemporary dilemmas, attitudes, research and technology. Bosworth Battlefield, Leicestershire, U.K., discussed. bib. illus.

218. Jacques, David. "What to Do About Earlier Inaccurate Restoration: A Case Study of Chiswick House Grounds." *APT Bulletin* 24, no.3&4 (1992): pp.4-13.

   Author responsible for site's gardens and grounds from 1987-1993. Restoration from 1950's compared to contemporary approaches. Chronology of plan views. illus.

219. Jamieson, Walter. "Recording the Historic Urban Environment: A New Challenge." *APT Bulletin* 22, no.1&2 (1990): pp.12-16.

   Components of urban districts, recording devices, processes discussed. Defining historic urban districts for preservation planning, and intervention purposes. Canadian perspective, applicable elsewhere. bib. illus.

220. Jamieson, Walter; Buchik, Pat. "Training in Historic Resource Management: The Development of an Approach for Western Canada." *APT Bulletin* 20, no.1 (1988): pp.50-61.

   Impact of personnel training on historic preservation; importance of multi-disciplinary approach. Fourteen areas of training activity described, including landscape design, building science and technology, interpretation, museum development. Training opportunies in Canada and abroad described. bib. illus.

221. Jarvis, Jonathan B. "Principles and Practices of a Research and Resource Management Program." *The George Wright Forum* 8, no.3 (1991): pp.2-11.

   Advice to National Park Service managers on link between scientific research and park units. Discussion of relationship between research and management; developing resource management programs.

222. Jester, Thomas C.; Park, Sharon C. *Making Historic Properties Accessible.*, U.S. Department of the Interior. National Park Service Cultural Resources. Preservation Assistance Division., Washington, D.C., 14 pp.

   Planning accessibility modifications and illustrated solutions. Overview of Federal Accessibility Law. Focus on structures, but includes "Making Historic Landscapes Accessible" (Charles A. Birnbaum). bib. illus.

223. Jones, Dwayne. "Developing a Survey Methodology for Roadside Resources." *CRM* 16, no.6 (1993): p.33.

   Benefits, disadvantages of three cultural resource survey methods applied to roadways, linear, thematic, and resource based.

224. Jones, Harvie P. "Enhancement of Historic Photographs." *APT Bulletin* 11, no.1 (1979): pp.4-12.

   Photographic enhancement using methods developed by National Aeronautics and Space Administration (NASA) and the Jet Propulsion Laboratory (JPL) of Pasadena, Calif., reveal otherwise invisible details in buildings, landscapes. illus.

225. Jones, Lucy E. "Collections Policy: The Basics." *The Public Garden* 1, no.3 (1986): pp.8-9,12.

Editorial; need for botanical gardens and arboreta to develop collections policy to guide management and define institutional goals. illus.

226. Jones-Roe, Charlotte; Shaw, Jonathan A. "Conservation in North American Gardens." *The Public Garden* 3, no.1 (1988): pp.25-27.

AABGA (American Association of Botanical Gardens and Arboreta) survey of how institutions promote plant conservation. Includes acquisition of rare and endangered plants, in situ conservation, rare plant propagation, in-house training and standards.

227. Journal Scientifique. Jardins et Sites Historiques., US ICOMOS, 1993. 377 pp.

A compilation of conference papers on the subject since the first congress held in Fontainebleau, 1971, to the Potsdam Meeting, 1989. Fifty-three papers in english and french, include the following english language contributions related specifically to planning and treatment: Special Problems Connected with the Conservation of Gardens of Historical Interest in Japan, M. Yokoyame; Problems of Garden Archaeology in the U.S.S.R., Elena Micoulina and Tochtahojaeva; Restoration of Historical Parks with Regard to Dendrological Issues, Pavol Simkovic; Conservation and value of the Galician Pazo, Carmen Pazo; Problems of Restoration and Preservation of Landscape Gardens, Detlef Karg; Interpretations of the English Language Garden, David Jacques; Garden Monument Conservation in Berlin as exemplified by the Hunting Lodge Park at Klein-Glienicke; Historical Country Residences in the Netherlands. Their Importance and Care, Robert deJong; Preservation of Historical Buildings and Gardens of the Dessau-Worlitz Reform Works, Helmut Stelzer. Includes Florence Charter. illus.

228. Kain, Roger J. P. "Conservation of Historic Gardens and Parks on the Continent of Europe: Italy, France, Belgium,

West Germany and Hungary." *Landscape Research* 12, no.2
(1987): pp.1-2.

Introduction to second thematic issue on conservation, author
contributions, addresses. Central European focus. illus.

229. Kane, Thomas J. "Cemetery Wall Restoration, New
Harmony, Indiana." *APT Bulletin* 9, no.3 (1977): pp.39-51.

The treatment of a free-standing brick wall. illus.

230. Kane, Thomas J. "The Crunch Underfoot." *APT Bulletin* 21,
no.1 (1989): pp.4-5.

The treatment of walks with stabilized earth, shells, and
crushed stones. illus.

231. Keister, Kim. "Shapers of the Landscape Heritage." *Historic
Preservation Forum* 33, no.2 (1993): pp.20-21.

National Trust announces $100,000 matching grant from
Henry Luce Foundation, N.Y.C. to research and document its
landscapes. Two sites which have initiated research discussed:
Shadows-on-the-Teche, New Iberia, La., and Lyndhurst,
Tarrytown, N.Y..

232. Keller, Genevieve P. "The Inventory and Analysis of Historic
Landscapes." *Historic Preservation Forum* 7, no.3 (1993):
pp.26-35.

Descriptions of inventory, documentation and analysis of
cultural landscapes. Discussion of National Park Service
programs, cultural landscape reports and state-wide landscape
surveys. illus.

233. Keller, J. Timothy; Keller, Genevieve P. *How to Evaluate
and Nominate Designed Historic Landscapes.*, U.S.
Department of the Interior. National Park Service Cultural
Resources. Interagency Resources Division., Washington,
D.C., 14 pp.

Guidance for successful preparation of nominations for
designed historic landscapes. Definitions and types. Field
work, research, documentation and assessment techniques.

Landscape archaeology. Step-by-step process for determining integrity and significance. National examples. bib. illus.

234. Kelley, K. Vance. "Kansas Law: Protecting the Environs of Historic Properties." *Historic Preservation Forum* 5, no.1 (1991): pp.4-5.

State of Kansas has historic preservation laws that include environs in addition to properties and sites.

235. Kelly, Deborah Marquis; Goodman, Jennifer. "Conservation Districts as an Alternative to Historic Districts." *Historic Preservation Forum* 7, no.5 (1993): pp.6-14.

Expanding concept of historic districts to encompass older, distinctive neighborhoods lacking significance used as a planning tool for neighborhood preservation in Philadelphia. bib. illus.

236. Kelly, Linda. "The National Road: A Story with Many Facets--A Road with Many Resources." *CRM* 16, no.11 (1993): pp.50-51,53.

Built between 1811-1838, the National Road spans six states. Contextual overview; development and evaluation of Pa. portion as prototype; integrity and significance evaluation. bib. illus.

237. Kelso, Gerald K. "The Kirk Street Agent's House, Lowell, Massachusetts: Interdisciplinary Analysis of the Historic Landscape." *Landscape Journal* 12, no.2 (1993): pp. 143-155.

Paleobotanical research to fill gaps in documentary and photographic records, chronicles changes over time at the Kirk Street Agent's House, Lowell, Mass. illus.

238. Kelso, Gerald K. "Pollen-Record Information Processes, Interdisciplinary Archeology and Land Use by Mill Workers and Managers: The Boott Mills Corporation, Lowell, Massachusetts, 1836-1942." *Historical Archaeology* 27, no.1 (1993): pp.70-94.

Archaeological, palynological study of nineteenth century mill worker boardinghouses and supervisor residences, when integrated with other data sources, generate socio-cultural, ideological historical interpretation. bib. illus.

239. Kelso, Gerald K.; Karish, John F.; Smith, C. "Pollen Analysis in Historical Landscape Studies: Fort Necessity, Pennsylvania." *Park Science* 13, no.2 (1993): pp.8-10.

Site of opening battle of French and Indian War, 1754. Soil core samples along transects used to determine forest, understory, herbaceous plant layers, and guide reconstruction. illus.

240. Kelso, William. "Why Are You Digging Way Out Here? The Role of Landscape Archaeology." *Courier* 34, no.8 (1989): pp.20-22.

Role of archaeology in garden history; importance of on-site interpretation. Carter's Grove Plantation, Williamsburg; Monticello, Charlottesville, Va., discussed. illus.

241. Kennedy, C. Barrett. "Videographic Documentation Analysis and Manipulation: A New Tool for Cultural Resource Management." *APT Bulletin* 22, no.1&2 (1990): pp.97-103.

Introduction to methodology; application to Section 106 of National Historic Preservation Act of 1966; interface with Computer Aided Design and Drafting (CADD) systems; advantages of visual simulation. bib. illus.

242. Kennedy, Roger. "A Letter from Friendship Hill." *The George Wright Forum* 10, no.2 (1993): pp.13-19.

Discussion of conservation of "natural" areas versus historic preservation of "cultural" resources; reinterpretation of Friendship Hill National Historic Site, near Pittsburgh, Pa., former home of Albert Gallatin (1761-1849), statesman, founder of U.S. Bureau of Ethnology. Native American earthworks, historic preservation addressed.

243. Kenyon, Jeff L. "Ground-Penetrating Radar and its Application to a Historical Archeological Site." *Historical Archaeology* 11, (1977): pp.48-55.

Describes Electromagnetic Subsurface Profiler (also called downward searching radar) at Stenton Mansion Complex,

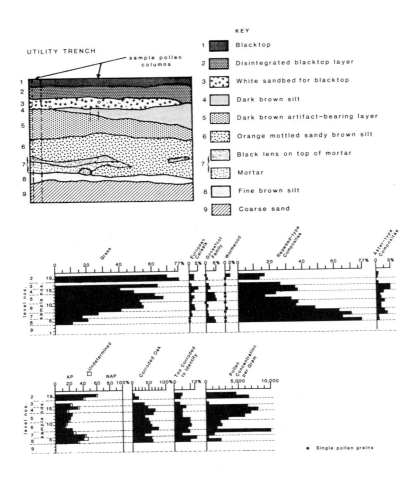

See citation 239: Gerald K. Kelso. "Pollen-Record Information Processes, Interdisciplinary Archeology and Land Use by Mill Workers and Managers: The Boott Mills Corporation, Lowell, Massachusetts, 1836-1942." *Historical Archaeology*, 1993. Kirk Street Agents' House: East profile of the utility trench showing location of pollen sample (top); and, Pollen percentages of critical types in the utility trench (bottom).

Philadelphia, Pa. This non-excavation survey device registers data from one to ten feet below the ground. Procedure, application to archaeology discussed. bib. illus.

244. Kilpinen, Jon T. "Traditional Fence Types of Western North America." *Pioneer America Society Transactions* 15, (1992): pp.15-22.

Description of traditional agricultural fencing and discussion of adaptation of eastern fences to accommodate western needs. Significance of fence in interpretation of western settlement landscape. bib. illus.

245. Kintish, Brian; Shapiro, John. "Neighborhood and Historic Preservation." *CRM* 15, no.8 (1992): pp. 11-13.

Economic value: historic districts and zoning; specific examples. Article is an excerpt from 1990 Municipal Art Society commissioned study by Abeles, Phillips, Preiss & Shapiro, N.Y.

246. Kirby, Valerie G. "Heritage or Millstone? A Review of the Relevance of Historic Landscapes in New Zealand Today." *The George Wright Forum* 11, no.1 (1994): pp.54-62.

Concepts of natural and cultural heritage among New Zealanders of European and Maori descent discussed. Importance of both cultural and ecological landscape components in developing sustainable landscape management strategy. bib.

247. Kitson, Ian. "A Country House Near Leicester" *Landscape Design* no.193 (Sept.'90): pp.22-26.

Professional career of Christopher Tunnard (1910-1979). Review and analysis of his plans for a property near Leicester, U.K., with insights into the design and future management. illus.

248. Koller, Gary L. "Arnold: An Accession Policy." *The Public Garden* 1, no.3 (1986): pp.10-12.

Arnold Arboretum, Jamaica Plain, Mass., plant collections policy maintains balance between acquisition and conservation; provides research resource. illus.

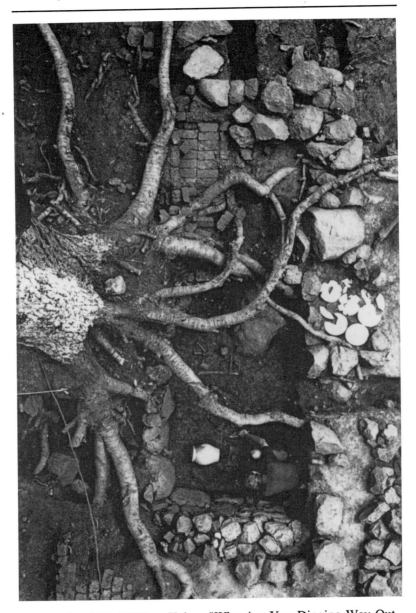

See citation 240: William Kelso. "Why Are You Digging Way Out
Here? The Role of Landscape Archaeology." *Courier*, 1989.
Overhead view of foundations of one of several slave quarters along
the original entrance road to Monticello.

249. Kottaridis, Kathy. "Interpreting Historic Burying Grounds: Boston's Initiative." *CRM* 17, no.7 (1994): pp.41-43.

Collaborative effort by Boston Parks, Boston Landmarks Commission and the Bostonian Society to preserve and manage nineteen historic cemeteries. Inventory of over 150,000 markers. Master plan completed in 1985. Interpretation and outreach programs include the 40-mile, one day "Tour de Grave" bicycle tour. bib. illus.

250. Krakow, Jere L. "Identifying and Evaluating Historic Corridors and Trails." *CRM* 16, no.11 (1993): pp.14, 20.

Advocates holistic approach to transportation corridor resources: archaeology, ethnology, geography, architecture and landscape architecture. Need to establishing contexts, surveys, registration, documentation, field work.

251. Krebs, Wolfgang. "The Historic Parks of Cleves and their Restoration." *Journal of Garden History* 6, no.4 (1986): pp.376-389.

Restoration of Netherlands site re-establishes relationship of parkland to development of the town and provides a recreational area accessible to the general public. bib. illus.

252. Krosigk, Klaus von. "Preservation and Maintenance of Historic Gardens and Parks in West Germany." *Landscape Research* 12, no.2 (1987): pp.18-21.

History and update of twentieth century government sponsored activities. bib. illus.

253. Kunst, Scott G.; Tucker, Arthur O. "'Where Have All the Flowers Gone?': A Preliminary List of Origination Lists for Ornamental Plants." *APT Bulletin* 21, no.2 (1989): pp.43-50.

Contains international, annotated bibliographic references arranged by common name of woody and herbaceous plant material. Establishes date(s), place(s) of introduction, availability, aesthetic value, uses during historic period. illus.

254. Laird, Mark. "Approaches to Planting in the Late Eighteenth Century: Some Imperfect Ideas on the Origins of the American

Garden." *Journal of Garden History* 11, no.3 (1991): pp.154-172.

Analysis of planting plans for flower beds at Hartwell. Author's watercolors of flower bed elevations based on these plans. Connections between Hartwell and Nuneham Courtenay gardens, U.K. bib. illus.

255. Laird, Mark. "'Our Equally Favorite Hobby Horse': The Flower Gardens of Lady Elizabeth Lee at Hartwell and the 2nd Earl Harcourt at Nuneham Courtenay." *Garden History* 18, no.2 (1990): pp.103-151.

Appendix I: Lord Harcourt's Letter. Appendix II: The Plants at Hartwell, U. K. 1799, identified by John Harvey. bib., annotated. illus.

256. Lamme, Ary J., III. "America's Historic Landscapes: Community Power and the Preservation of Four National Historic Sites." Knoxville, Tennessee: The University of Tennessee Press, 1989. 213 pp.

Landscape and meaning, including a review of literature. Analysis of historic landscapes; "contemplative" analysis of landscape meaning; and, community perspectives. Eastern U.S. case studies: St. Augustine, Fla.; Colonial National Historical Park, Va.; Sackets Harbor, N.Y.; and, Gettysburg, Pa. Review of findings and strategies. bib. illus.

257. Land Trust Alliance; The National Trust for Historic Preservation in the United States. "Appraising Easements: Guidelines for Valuation of Historic Preservation and Land Conservation Easements." 2d ed. Land Trust Alliance and the National Trust for Historic Preservation in the United States, 1990. 82 pp.

The process of easement appraisal. Includes the general principles of valuation, guidelines for appraisal reports, use of professional appraisal approaches, typical easements, and the role of the holding organization. bib.

258. "Landscape and Garden Preservation in New England: Current Research and Garden Restorations." *The Labyrinth* 1, no.1 (1990): pp.4-15.

Updates on: Morrill Homestead, Strafford, Vt., Jekyll Garden at Glebe House, Woodbury, Conn., Strawberry Banke, Portsmouth, N.H., John Hay Estate, Lake Sunapee, N.H., and others.

259. Landscape Preservation Seminar. University of Massachusetts at Amherst, 25-26 March 1988. University of Massachusetts at Amherst: Division of Continuing Education, 1988. 89 pp.

Parts Cars, Green Roofs, and 1990s Landscape Preservation, John R. Stilgoe; Inventory and Evaluation: Historic Landscapes in the National Register, Linda Flint McClelland; Inventory and Evaluation of Historic Landscapes: The State Level, Katherine Boonin; Acknowledging the "Who" Factor: A Challenge at the Local Level, Ann L. Marston; Preservation of New Hampshire Estate Gardens: What Remains of What Was, Lucinda A. Brockway; Private Residences as National Historic Sites: Issues and Opportunities in Landscape Management, Nora J. Mitchell and Dwight T. Pitcaithley; Landscape Preservation and Economic Development: A New Battleground? John R. Mullin; Town Character: Towards a Useable Definition, Elizabeth Brabec; Rural Landscape Planning in the Connecticut River Valley of Massachusetts, Robert D. Yaro and Randall Arendt; The Politics of Landscape Preservation, Susan Quateman; Where Am I Now? Regionalism and Rural Landscape Protection, Robert Z. Melnick; Landscape Preservation: What's Next, Hugh C. Miller.

260. le Vicomte de Noailles. "The Protection of Historic Gardens in France." *Garden History* 3, no.4 (1975): pp.48-49.

National laws affecting garden preservation discussed. National examples.

261. Leach, Sara Amy. "Documenting Rock Creek and Potomac Parkway." *CRM* 16, no.3 (1993): pp.5-7.

Pilot project producing drawings photographs, written narratives. Development of digitized mapping and interpretive drawings from photogrammetric photographs. illus.

262. Leach, Sara Amy. "HABS/HAER Documents Automotive Corridors." *CRM* 16, no.11 (1993): pp.26-27.

   Documentation of park roads, parkways, urban thoroughfares. Rock Creek Parkway, George Washington Memorial Parkway, L'Enfant-McMillan Plan, Washington, D.C., Merritt Parkway, Conn., discussed. bib. illus.

263. Leach, Sara Amy. "Made for Motoring." *CRM* 16, no.6 (1993): pp.40-42.

   1992 HABS/HAER documentation projects compared: Rock Creek and Potomac Parkway, Washington, D.C. and the Merritt Parkway, N.Y. and Conn. Use of written histories, original and contemporary photographs and drawings to rehabilitate and restore original appearance. illus.

264. Lee, Ellen. "A Piggy-Back Approach to Archeological Resource Inventory." *APT Bulletin* 22, no.1&2 (1990): pp.17-20.

   Pilot project attempts integration of Archaeological Resource Inventory with Natural Resource Management Process of Canadian National Parks through wardens' field work, computer geographic information system. Goals: predict location of archaeological sites in unsurveyed areas; monitor known sites for natural and human disturbance. illus.

265. Lemmon, Ken. "Restoration at Studley Royal." *Garden History* 1, no.1 (1972): pp.22-23.

   Late eighteenth century estate undergoes restoration, funded by new owners, West Riding County Council. Vegetation renewal to open historic vistas, restoration of follies, grottos, garden furniture discussed. illus.

266. Letellier, Robin. "Heritage Recording: An Essential Activity within the Conservation Process of Historic Resources." *APT Bulletin* 18, no.1&2 (1986): pp.109-111.

   Parks Canada's Heritage Recording Management System (HRMS) to produce reliable records of historic resources for conservation studies and posterity. Scope of work, clients, types of documentation, training of field personnel, outlined. bib.

267. Letellier, Robin. "ICOMOS Canada's Recording and Documentation Committee." *APT Bulletin* 22, no.1&2 (1990): pp.93-96.

RDC committee established 1983; subsequent series of workshops establish goals, objectives, methodology. Introduction of the "Inventory and Location of Original Records System" (ILORS), a computerized technical documents management database started in 1985 by the Heritage Recording Services of Parks Canada.

268. Lewis, Peirce. "Common Landscapes as Historic Documents., in "History from Things: Essays on Material Culture." Lubar, Steven and Kingery, W. David, eds. Washington, D.C.: Smithsonian Institution Press, 1993. pp. 115-139.

Cultural geographer's perspective on reading the cultural landscape. Bellefonte, Pa., case study reveals the wealth of information contained in the surviving fabric of an ordinary American small town landscape. Direct observation techniques. Benefits and limitations of approach. bib. illus.

269. Lewis, Peirce. "Learning From Looking: Geographic and Other Writing About the American Cultural Landscape." *American Quarterly* 35, no.3 (1983): pp.242-261.

Recognition of scholars from recent time: Carl O. Sauer, Fred B. Kniffen, John K. Wright and J.B. Jackson. Analytical review of current body of literature and contemporary approaches.

270. Lewis, Peirce. "Taking Down the Velvet Rope: Cultural Geography and the Human Landscape.", in "Past Meets Present: Essays about Historic Interpretation and Public Audiences." Blatti, Jo, ed. Washington, D.C.: Smithsonian Institution Press, 1987. pp. 23-29.

Cultural geographer's perspective on landscape as artifact. Author cites need to suspend aesthetic value judgements and to recognize that history and geography are dimensions, not things. bib.

271. Lidfors, Kate. "Preserving Alaska's Landscape is Preserving the Human Touch." *Courier* 34, no.8 (1989): pp.16-18.

Need to inventory, protect, interpret Alaska's cultural landscape features. illus.

272. Liebs, Chester H. "Reconnecting People with Place." *CRM* 16, no.11 (1993): pp.9-11.

Stewardship of transportation corridors in historic preservation context. Case study: Jamaica Avenue, Brooklyn and Queens, N.Y., N.Y. Prospects and global perspective. bib.

273. Lind, Brenda. "The Conservation Easement Stewardship Guide: Designing, Monitoring, and Enforcing Easements" Washington, D.C.: Land Trust Alliance, 1991. 107 pp.

Establishing a program, accepting, documenting, monitoring, enforcing and funding easements. Property owner and community relations. Appendices: rules for record keeping; sample survey and documentation forms; and, sample policies. illus.

274. Linden-Ward, Blanche. "Stan Hywet." *Landscape Architecture* 77, no.4 (1987): pp.66-71.

Stan Hywet Hall, Akron, Ohio, 1911-1956; landscape history, influence of Warren Manning (designer) and Frank Sieberling (owner). Current planning and treatment response to fifty year decline of vegetation and vistas. bib. illus.

275. Lindley, Christopher. "Rochester and its River: A Unifying Gift of Nature." *Trends* 29, no.2 (1992): pp.5-12.

Four-year planning process for the South River Corridor Managment Plan. History of Genessee River (N.Y.) and its role in multiple-partner initiative. Accomplishments over past decade. illus.

276. Lipsey, Ellen J. "Boston's Historic Burying Grounds." *APT Bulletin* 21, no.2 (1989): pp.6-9.

Describes objectives, methodologies, funding, for 1985 Master Plan for all sixteen sites under jurisdiction of Boston Parks and Recreation Department. Treatment options, accomplishments to date. illus.

277. Loeb, Robert E. "Long Term Arboreal Change in a Landscaped Urban Park: Central Park, New York." *Journal of Arboriculture* 19, no.4 (1993): pp.238-249.

Historical records of the forest composition, structure and environment of Central Park examined to determine long term forest changes, contributing factors. bib.

278. Lombaerde, Piet. "The Conservation of Historic Parks and Landscape Gardens in Belgium: Examples from Enghien, Brussels and Antwerp." *Landscape Research* 12, no.2 (1987): pp.13-17.

Preservation strategy for privately owned properties. Sixteenth to nineteenth century history and treatment chronology on Enghien, the Parc Ducal, Parc Royal in Brussels, and the Parc de la Ville, Antwerp. bib. illus.

279. Longstrength, Richard. "The Significance of the Recent Past." *APT Bulletin* 23, no.2 (1991): pp.7-24.

Contemporary critical acclaim versus historic value; attribution of historic significance to mid-twentieth century properties, especially urban commercial sites, discussed. Fifty year provision for National Register designation; exception of Dulles International Airport, Washington, D.C., addressed. National examples. bib. illus.

280. Low, Setha M. "Cultural Diversity and Place Preservation." *CRM* 16, no.11 (1993): pp.31-33.

Historic corridors and cultural resources. Influences of politics, pluralism, and cultural change on the landscape. Preservation methodologies and strategies. bib. illus.

281. Lowenthal, David. "Historic Landscapes: Indispensable Hub, Interdisciplinary Orphan." *Landscape Research* 15, no.2 (1990): pp.27-29.

Historical qualities in landscapes and their cultural variations. Preservation planning neglect in U.K. New planning terms: 'areas of outstanding natural beauty, sites of special scientific interest, environmentally sensitive areas.' Preservation rationales.

282. Lucas, P. C. London, U.K.: Chapman and Hall, 1992. 90pp.

    International case studies; planning and management tools.
    Appendix: International directory of protected areas
    management agencies. Protected Landscapes: A guide for
    Policy-Makers and Planners. bib. illus.

283. Luxenberg, Gretchen. "Interpreting Ebey's Landing National
    Historical Reserve." *CRM* 17, no.7 (1994): pp.44-47.

    Interpreting change at 17,400 acre Puget Sound, Wa. cultural
    landscape for community and park visitors. Tools
    implemented by National Park Service based on "Interpretive
    Prospectus" and "Wayside Exhibit Plan." Twelve sites
    selected in partnership with Island County and Wash. state
    agencies (e.g. use of scenic easements.) Role of signs, kiosks
    and drive and/or bicycle tours to educate and orient. bib.
    illus.

284. MacGregor, Molly. "The Mississippi Headwaters Board."
    Historic Preservation Forum 6, no.2 (1992): pp.33-39.

    Mississippi Headwaters Board, an inter-jurisdictional
    planning board, given zoning authority to preserve and protect
    the River's Minn. corridor.

285. Maney-O'Leary, Susan. "Preserving and Managing Design
    Intent in Historic Landscapes." *The Public Garden* 7, no.2
    (1992): pp.14-17.

    Questionaire intended as tool for board members,
    committees, staff of public historic designed landscapes.
    Design intent, archives, user groups, maintenance and
    documentation discussed. illus.

286. Manshel, Andrew M. "Bryant Park: A Model for the
    Future." *The Public Garden* 8, no.1 (1993): pp. 13-17.

    Public/private partnership restores historic N.Y.C. park and
    ensures future maintenance and operation. illus.

287. Marshall, E. Timothy. "Construction and Maintenance of
    Rustic Furnishings, Central Park, New York." *CRM* 16, no.4
    (1993): pp. 32-34.

Park history and preservation planning; in-house project implementation by 'restoration crew.' Skill development, training and project examples. illus.

288. Marshall, J. M. "Computerisation of Landscape Surveys." *APT Bulletin* 15, no.4 (1983): pp.55-56.

Surveys of National Trust U.K. properties for the purpose of producing accurate scale plans; written reports based on archival research; indexing all woody plants on site. Data transferred to computer database. bib.

289. Martin, Frank Edgerton ,. ed. "A History of Minnesota Landscape Architecture: Measuring Our History and its Lessons for the Future." *Minnesota Common Ground* 1, no.No.2 (1994): pp.1-2.

Twenty page thematic issue by Minn. landscape architects to understand regional history and establish a foundation for present day planning and design. Related styles and historical figures.

290. Mason, Randall J. "An Unorthodox Magnetic Survey of a Large Forested Historic Site." *Historical Archaeology* 18, no.2 (1984): pp.54-63.

Tombigbee Historic Townsites Project explores nineteenth century river-town, Barton, Miss. Proton magnetometers used in survey. Excavation and magnetic survey yield unexpectedly few structural feature remains. illus.

291. Masson, Georgina. "Garden Restoration in Italy." *Garden History* 3, no.4 (1975): pp.45-47.

Role of archaeology in historic garden preservation since the late nineteenth, early twentieth centuries; survey of early twentieth century preservation efforts; need to comprehensive nation-wide historic garden survey and preservation funding.

292. Mastran, Shelley S. "A Community Rescue Team." *Historic Preservation Forum* 6, no.3 (1992): pp.41-47.

A U.S./U.K. team barnstorms and brainstorms on rural and agricultural preservation in Long Island town of North Fork.

See citation 287: E. Timothy Marshall. "Construction and Maintenance of Rustic Furnishings, Central Park, New York." *CRM*, 1993 Rustic carpentry techniques.

293. Mastran, Shelley S. "A Look at Greenways." *Historic Preservation Forum* 6, no.2 (1992): pp.13-30.

   Overview of preservation of corridor or linear systems including trails, scenic byways, rural roads, greenways, highways, heritage and river corridors.

294. Mastran, Shelley S. *The Protection of America's Scenic Byways.*, National Trust for Historic Preservation, Washington, D.C., 1993. 20 pp.

   Overview of federal and state programs. Threats from tourism and urban sprawl. Preservation planning tools: Corridor Management Plans and incentive programs. Case studies: Lexington-Frankfort, Ky. Scenic Corridor; Red Hills Regions of Ga. and Fla; Brandywine River Valley, Pa; and Columbia River Highway, Oreg. bib., annotated. illus.

295. Mastran, Shelley S. *Rural Conservation.*, National Trust for Historic Preservation, Washington, D.C., 1993. 24 pp.

   Development pressures. Rural, economic, demographic and social problems. Initiating and managing a program. Inventory and analysis of natural and cultural features. Land protection techniques: zoning, regulating subdivision. Voluntary techniques: notification and recognition, acquisition, tax incentives, right of first refusal, leasebacks. Opportunities and sources of assistance. bib., annotated. illus.

296. Matero, Frank G.; Bass, Angelyn. "Orphans of the Storm: The Preservation of Architectural Plasters in Eastern Ruins." *CRM* 17, no.4 (1994): pp. 21-26.

   Contemporary treatment offers new possibilities for in situ stabilization, interpretation. Documentation, treatment descriptions. Glossary of technical terms. Case studies: Fort Union National Monument, N.Mex., Fort Davis National Historic Site, Tex. illus.

297. Mathien, Frances Joan. "Chalmette National Historic Park: A Remote Sensing Project." *Historical Archaeology* 15, no.2 (1981): pp.69-86.

Black and white, color infrared photography, and
multispectral imagery compared. Color infrared photography
favored for studying wet lowland sites. illus.

298. Matthews, Russel. "Polishing Up the Necklace" *Landscape
Design* no.180 (May '89): pp.19-22.

Inventory of existing conditions, Boston's Emerald Necklace;
management options; comparisons between U.S. and U.K.
park maintenance. illus.

299. Mayall, R. Newton. "Recording Historic American Landscape
Architecture." *Landscape Architecture* 26, no.1 (1935):
pp.1-11.

Historic perspective of early Historic American Buildings
Survey (HABS) project to document colonial Mass. gardens.
bib. illus.

300. McClelland, Linda Flint and; Keller, J. Timothy; Keller,
Genevieve P.; Melnick, Robert Z. *Guidelines for Evaluating
and Documenting Rural Historic Landscapes.*, U.S.
Department of the Interior. National Park Service Cultural
Resources. Interagency Resources Division., Washington,
D.C., 33 pp.

Guidance for successful preparation of nominations for
rural/historic landscapes. Definitions and types. Field work,
documentation and assessment techniques. Landscape
archaeology. Matrix of landscape characteristics.
Step-by-step process for determining integrity and significance.
National examples. bib. illus.

301. McClelland, Linda Flint. "What does the National Register
Do for Landscapes?" *Courier* 34, no.8 (1989): p.25.

Created in 1966, the National Historic Preservation Act's
National Register includes National Park Service landscapes.

302. McCormick, Kathleen. "Vaulting the Garden Wall."
Landscape Architecture 84, no.5 (1994): pp.74-81.

Changing attitudes in landscape preservation. National
perspectives, new standards and technologies. Project

summaries: Olmsted National Historic Site, Brookline, Mass.;
Shadows-on-the Teche, New Iberia, La.; Rancho Los
Alamitos, Long Beach, Calif.; Acadia National Park, Mt.
Desert Island, Maine. illus.

303. McDaniel, J. C. "Fitting Species and Cultivars to the
Landscape" *Landscape Architecture* 66, no.3 (1976): pp.
267-269.

The treatment of historic plants materials including substitute
and in-kind replacement. illus.

304. McDonald, Travis C. ,. Jr. "Restoration, Re-Restoration and
Real History." *Historic Preservation Forum* 7, no.6 (1993):
pp.21-26.

Restoration of historic house museums is both a product and
process. Interpretation for the public and historical accuracy
are equally important.

305. McDonnell, Mark J. "A Forest for New York." *The Public
Garden* 3, no.2 (1988): pp.28-31.

General philosophy for the preservation, management of
historic natural landscapes. illus.

306. McGann, Martin R. "Maintaining the Historic Garden." *The
Public Garden* 4, no.3 (1989): pp.22-25,38.

Maintenance methods, machinery, use of heirloom plants,
historic garden personnel training discussed. illus.

307. McGann, Martin R. "Securing the Plant Link." *Landscape
Architecture* 77, no.4 (1987): pp.91-92.

Historic plant materials resources: reliability, heirloom plant
specialists, collections. Historic site plant collection
management. Examples: Bacon's Castle, Richmond, Va.,
Philipsburg Manor, Tarrytown, N.Y., and Monticello,
Charlottesville, Va. Source list. bib. illus.

308. McGowen, Keven P.; Lautenschlager, Eric. "Nineteenth
Century Agricultural Drainage Technology in the Midwest."
Material Culture 20, no.3 (1988): pp.57-67.

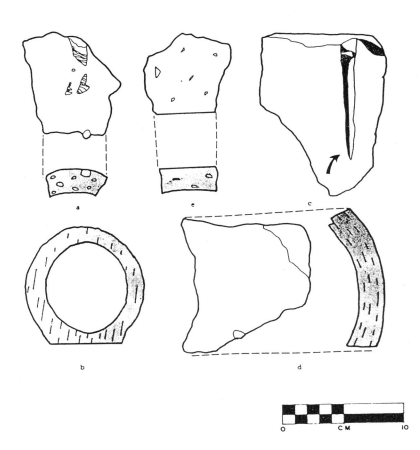

See citation 308: Kevin P. McGowen and Eric Lautenschlager. "Nineteenth Century Agricultural Drainage Technology in the Midwest." *Material Culture*, 1988. Discerning manufacturing marks on drainage tiles: (a) grog temper; (b) wire cut marks; (c) die marks; (d) clay layering; and, (e) chert temper marks.

Ceramic drainage tile design, production, installation discussed. Examples from Illinois. bib. illus.

309. McGuire, Diane Kostial. "Garden Planning for Continuity at Dumbarton Oaks." *Landscape Architecture* 71, no.1 (1981): pp.82-85.

Maintenance and management for historic gardens as illustrated in D.C. estate landscape designed by Beatrix Farrand. illus.

310. McMahon, Edward T. "Saving Our Sense of Place." *Historic Preservation Forum* 5, no.1 (1991): pp.30-35.

Protecting and preserving local character and 'sense of place' requires an overall approach including viewshed protection, heritage corridors, gateways and sign control. illus.

311. McMahon, Edward T.; Watson, A. Elizabeth. *In Search of Collaboration: Historic Preservation and the Environmental Movement.*, National Trust for Historic Preservation, Washington, D.C., 1992. 16 pp.

Exploration of common roots, interests, and problems: energy conservation, urban environment, transportation, tourism, greenways and heritage corridors. Opportunites: sustainable development, partnerships, sharing tools, planning and programs. Case studies: Lancaster County, Pa.; Bodie State Park, Calif.; Fenstermarker Ranch, San Antonio, Tex. illus.

312. Medbury, Scott. "Taxonomy and Arboretum Design." *Arnoldia* 53, no.3 (1993): pp.13-23.

History of development of sequentially ordered taxonomic nineteenth century plant collections. Historic plans. illus.

313. Meier, Lauren G. ed. *Historic Landscape Directory: A Source Book of Agencies, Organizations, and Institutions Providing Information on Historic Landscape Preservation.*, U.S. Department of the Interior. National Park Service Cultural Resources. Preservation Assistance Division. In collaboration with The Catalog of Landscape Records in the United States,

Wave Hill and US ICOMOS Historic Landscapes Committee, Washington, D.C., 96 pp.

National organizations and regional organizations by state. Educational programs, libraries, archives, computerized directories, journals and sources of information on historic plant materials. bib. illus.

314. Meier, Lauren G. "The Treatment of Historic Plant Material." *The Public Garden* 7, no.2 (1992): pp.24-27.

Describes categories of vegetation treatment consistent with the U.S. Secretary of the Interior's Standards for historic preservation projects. illus.

315. Meier, Lauren G.; Mitchell, Nora J. "Principles for Preserving Historic Plant Material." *CRM* 13, no.6 (1990): pp.17-24.

Importance of vegetation as character-defining feature of historic landscapes; processes for inventory, documentation, analysis, treatment; discussion of protection, preservation, restoration as applied to vegetation in historic landscapes. bib. illus.

316. Meinig, D.W., ed. "The Interpretation of Ordinary Landscapes." New York and Oxford: Oxford University Press, 1979. 255 pp.

Essays include: Axioms for Reading the Landscape: Some Guides to the American Scene, Peirce F. Lewis; The Beholding Eye: Ten Versions of the Same Scene, D.W. Meinig; The Biography of Landscape: Cause and Culpability, Marwyn S. Samuels; Thought and Landscape: The Eye and the Mind's Eye, Yi-Fu Tuan; Age and Artifact: Dilemmas of Appreciation, David Lowenthal; The Landscape of Home: Myth, Experience, Social Meaning, David E. Sopher; The Order of a Landscape: Reason and Religion and Newtonian America, J.B. Jackson; Symbolic Landscapes: Models of American Community, D.W. Meinig; Reading the Landscape: An Appreciation of W.G. Hoskins and J.B. Jackson. bib. illus.

317. Melnick, Robert Z. with; Sponn, Daniel and; Saxe, Emma Jane. "Cultural Landscapes: Rural Historic Districts in the National Park Service" Washington, D.C.: National Park Service, 1984.

Identification, evaluation, registration, and management of rural landscapes including its features, components and patterns. Contents of a Cultural Landscape Report. Appendicies: Standards for managing cultural resources (NPS-28); definitions, sources or information. bib., annotated. illus.

318. Melnick, Robert Z. "Capturing the Cultural Landscape." *Landscape Architecture* 71, no.1 (1981): pp.56-60.

Preservation planning and evaluating historic landscapes. Summary of findings from "Cultural Landscapes: Rural Historic Districts in the National Park System." illus.

319. Melnick, Robert Z. "Cultural and Historic Landscapes: A Selected Bibliography." Washington, D.C.: National Park Service, 1980.

Organized in seven sections: architecture, geography, historic preservation, landscape, planning, miscellaneous, and related bibliographies. Focus on vernacular and rural landscape information contained in journals.

320. Melnick, Robert Z. "Landscape Thinking." *CRM* 8, no.1 (1985): pp.1-2.

Evaluating integrity for historic rural landscapes. illus.

321. Melnick, Robert Z. "Preserving Cultural and Historic Landscapes: Developing Standards." *CRM* 3, no.1 (1980): pp.1-7.

Contemporary recognition to develop standards, guidance, and a common language. Definitions. illus.

322. Melnick, Robert Z. "Protecting Rural Cultural Landscapes: Finding Value in the Countryside." *The George Wright Forum* 3, no.1 (1983): pp.15-30.

See citation 325: Robert Z. Melnick and J. Timothy Keller. "Containing Tourism in Historic Hawaii." *Landscape Architecture*, 1987. Hanalei, on the north shore of the island of Kauai, is set within an ahupua'a, a traditional Hawaiian land division. Seen here are rural lands patterned by taro patches, irrigation ditches and farmhouses.

Defines "natural," "cultural," "historic" landscapes; lists components, social, political, economic factors affecting them; evaluation methods, determination of significance. bib.

323. Melnick, Robert Z. "Protecting Rural Cultural Landscapes: Finding Value in the Countryside." *Landscape Journal* 2, no.2 (1983): pp.85-91.

Documenting, evaluating and analyzing the components of a cultural landscape, including its context, organization and features. Determining significance. illus.

324. Melnick, Robert Z.; O'Donnell, Patricia M. "Toward a Preservation Ethic." *Landscape Architecture* 77, no.4 (1987): p.136.

Recent developments in theory and approach. Cultural resource values and landscape preservation.

325. Melnick, Robert Z.; Keller, J. Timothy. "Containing Tourism in Historic Hawaii." *Landscape Architecture* 77, no.4 (1987): pp.46-51.

Planning tools for rural landscapes. Balancing natural, scenic and cultural resources. Hanalei Valley, Kauai, case study: history, project overview, broader implications. illus.

326. Miller, Hugh C. "A New Direction for Civil War Battlefields, Historic Landscapes, and Rural Preservation." *Historic Preservation Forum* 5, no.1 (1991): pp.16-17.

U.S. Department of the Interior's American Battlefield Protection Program initiated in 1990 is intended to provide guidance including federal, state, and local assistance.

327. Miller, Hugh C. "Rural Landscaping." *CRM* 10, no.6 (1987): pp.1-3.

Comparison of cultural landscape preservation activities in the U.S. and U.K. The need for public-private partnerships in rural areas. illus.

328. Miller, Naomi F. "Palm Trees in Paradise: Victorian Views of the Ancient Near Eastern Landscape." *Expedition (The*

*University Magazine of Archaeology and Anthropology,
University of Pennsylvania)* 32, no.2 (1990): pp.52-61.

Vegetation in nineteenth, twentieth century paintings and
illustrated children's bible stories of ancient Near East
landscapes falsely depicted, despite new research on ancient
plant identification. bib. illus.

329. Miller, Naomi F.; Gleason, Kathryn Louise. "The
Archeology of Garden and Field." Philadelphia: University of
Pennsylvania Press, 1994.

Papers include: To Bound and to Cultivate: An Introduction
to the Archaeology of Gardens and Fields, Kathryn L.
Gleason; Fertilizer in the Identification and Analysis of
Cultivated Soil, Naomi F. Miller and Kathryn L. Gleason;
Archaeological Palynology of Gardens and Fields, Bruce
Bevan; The Creation of Cultivable Land Through Terracing,
John M. Treacy and William M. Denevan; Methodological
Consideration in the Study of Ancient Andean Field Systems,
Clark L. Erickson; The "Celtic" Field Systems on the
Berkshire Downs, England, Stephen Ford, Mark Bowden,
Vincent Gaffney and Geoffrey C. Mees; Techniques for
Excavating and Analyzing Buried Eighteenth-Century Garden
Landscapes, Anne E. Yentsch and Judson M. Kratzer; The
Landscapes and Ideational Roles of Caribbean Slave Gardens,
Lydia Mihelic Pulsipher. bib. illus.

330. Millman, Roger. "The Future of Historic Landscapes."
Landscape Research 4, no.3 (1979): get pp. from D.O. copy.

Training lay-people in the U.K. in landscape and
conservation methods. Case study: Hertfordshire, U.K..
Focus on settlement types and field patterns. illus.

331. Millstein, Cydney. "Kansas City's Park and Open Space
Legacy." *CRM* 16, no.4 (1993): pp.5-6,9.

Survey of 120 parks and boulevards designed and constructed
from 1893-1940. Impact of findings on current master plan
for 1,700 acre Swope Park. bib. illus.

See citation 329: Naomi F.Miller and Kathryn L. Gleason. *The Archeology of Garden and Field*, 1994. This open area excavation in courtyard of the Roman villa at Fishbourne revealed a central path, elaborate bedding trenches, and pits for espaliered (?) trees and supporting posts.

332. Mitchell, Nora J.; Page, Robert R. "Managing the Past for the Future." *Historic Preservation Forum* 7, no.3 (1993): pp.46-61.

Strategies for developing a landscape management program for dynamic landscape resources. Several National Park Service examples, including issues of vegetation, interpretation and traditional land uses. bib. illus.

333. Moggridge, Hal. "Notes on Kent's Garden at Rousham." *Journal of Garden History* 6, no.3 (1986): pp.187-226.

Discussion of lesser-known features of William Kent's 1740 design at Rousham, U.K., including an interpretation of the original plantings and water features. illus.

334. Moggridge, Hal. "The Working Method of Planting by which the Original Composition of Planting around L. Brown's Lakes was Defined." *Landscape Research* 9, no.2 (1984): pp.16-23.

Study of visual and spatial relationships around lakes at Blenheim, U.K.. Historic overview, visual analysis, studies and chronology with descriptions of extant graphic documentation. bib. illus.

335. Montagna, Dennis R. *Conserving Outdoor Bronze Sculpture.*, U.S. Department of the Interior. National Park Service Cultural Resources. Preservation Assistance Division., Washington, D.C., 1989. 8 pp.

Treatment case study of the Thaddeus Kosciuszko Monument, Wash., D.C. with air abrasive cleaning with pulverized walnut shells, followed by applications of corrosion inhibitor and protective wax coatings. Suggestions for maintenance and later evaluations. bib. illus.

336. Mughal, M. Rafique ,. Dr. "Preliminary Investigations for the Conservation and Restoration of Brick Pavement at Jahangir's Tomb, Lahore." *Lahore Museum Bulletin* 3, no.1 (1990): pp.79-87.

Case study of brick walkways in Mughal period garden (1526-1759) of Dilkusha, Pakistan. Test pit over walkway leading to Emperor's tomb (c.1637) excavated to determine

method of construction, dating, causes of deterioration.
Findings, recommendations. illus.

337. Murphy, Jean Parker; Ottavino, Kate Burns. "The
Rehabilitation of Bethesda Terrace." *APT Bulletin* 18, no.3
(1986): pp.24-39.

Central Park treatment project. Material testing, stone
specifications, graffiti removal, consolidation and
documentation, pavement rehabilitation, chronology of
terrace's landscape development, planting proposals. illus.

338. Murtagh, William J. "Landscape Preservation in Keeping
Time: The History and Theory of Preservation in America."
Pittstown, New Jersey: The Main Street Press, William Case
House, 1988.

Definitions, preservation planning considerations and national
examples. bib. illus.

339. Neal, Darwena. "Restoration of Designed Historic
Landscapes." *Courier* 34, no.8 (1989): pp.26-30.

Two early twentieth century Washington, D.C. gardens
discussed: Meridian Hill Park and Dumbarton Oaks Park.
Design intent, past and contemporary documentation,
vegetation renewal, maintenance addressed. bib. illus.

340. Neave, David. "Lord Burlington's Park and Gardens at
Londesborough, Yorkshire." *Garden History* 8, no.1 (1980):
pp.69-90.

History of the gardens at Londesborough, concentrating on
the eighteenth century era of Lord Burlington and comparisons
with his Chiswick property. illus.

341. *New Directions in Rural Preservation.*, U.S. Department of the
Interior. Heritage Conservation and Recreation Service.,
Washington, D.C., 1980. 115 pp.

Issues, techniques and tools in rural preservation. Papers
include: Federal Initiatives in Rural Preservation, Robert L.
Herbst; Rural Preservation: A Perpective and Challenge,
Robert E. Stipe; The Role of Rural Preservation in
Tomorrow's Rural Landscape, William H. Tishler; The

Vanishing Swimming Hole: Policy and Planning Perspectives on Rural Recreation, Ellen Ruth Reiss; Some Social and Economic Underpinnings of Rural Preservation, Ann Satterthwaite; Folklife and Cultural Preservation, Alan Jabbour and Howard W Marshall; Rural Historic Resources and the National Register, Bruce MacDougal; Federal Funds for Historic Preservation in Rural Areas, Marilyn P. Cable, Ken Pribanic, Barbara Hightower Fallin; Federal Programs to Preserve Natural and Recreation Resources in Rural America, Barry S. Tindall; The Role of Government in Shaping the Rural Landscape, Dallas D. Miner; Vernont Act 250 as a Tool for Rural Preservation, Chester H. Liebs; Private Rural Conservation Efforts, Samuel N. Stokes, A. Elizabeth Watson, Joe Getty, Douglas R. Horne; New Directions in Landscape Conservation and Informal Recreation in Britain, R.J.S. Hookway. bib. illus.

342. Newcomb, Robert M. "Planning the Past: Historical Landscape Resources and Recreation." Kent, U.K.: WM. Dawson & Sons Ltd., 1979.bib. illus.

343. Nichols, Susan. "Saving Outdoor Sculpture: A Nationwide Survey is Underway." *CRM* 16, no.5 (1993): pp.6-8.

Summary of program underway in forty-three states and Washington, D.C. Inventory and evaluation, volunteer training and executing survey forms. illus.

344. Nielsen, Erik Heeser. "The Danish Churchyard." *Landscape Design* no. 184 (Oct.'89): pp.33-36.

Burial grounds in Denmark, pre-historic to modern. illus.

345. Noble, Bruce J. Jr; Spude, Robert. *Guidelines for Identifying, Evaluating, and Registering Historic Mining Properties.*, U.S. Department of the Interior. National Park Service Cultural Resources. Interagency Resources Division., Washington, D.C., 1992. 30 pp.

Background and contexts for mining. Guidance for successful preparation of nominations. Description of processes: extraction, beneficiation and refining. Related property type descriptions. Field work, setting boundaries,

Step-by-step process for determining integrity and significance.
bib. illus.

346. Nowak, Timothy R. "Techniques of Identifying and
Evaluating Corridors and Trails: Archaeological Property
Types as Contributing Elements." *CRM* 16, no.11 (1993):
pp.12-13.

Above and below-ground remains linking the resource to its
context. Variables include assemblage, feature form and
location. Documentation of individual components (e.g. stone
fence lines, trail ruts) and integrity determination. Prescriptive
process.

347. Nunnally, Patrick. "Integrated Resource Management."
Historic Preservation Forum 7, no.2 (1993): pp. 36-40.

Rural preservation requires a management approach that
integrates the various resources, historic preservation programs
with working landscapes in order to promote economic
viability.

349. O'Donnell, Patricia M. "Cultural Landscape Analysis: the
Vanderbilt Estate at Hyde Park." *APT Bulletin* 24, no.3&4
(1992): pp.25-41.

Analysis of Hudson River, N.Y., estate. Graphic
documentation, inventory methodologies and strategies
applicable to sites of various scales and property sizes.
Determination of significance and integrity analysis. bib.
illus.

350. O'Donnell, Patricia M. "A Preservationist's Glossary."
Landscape Architecture 77, no.4 (1987): pp.96-98.

Landscape preservation glossary, landscape types, general
terms, and definitions. List of related disciplines and
interested parties.

351. O'Donnell, Patricia M. "A Process for Parks." *Landscape
Architecture* 77, no.4 (1987): pp. 56-61.

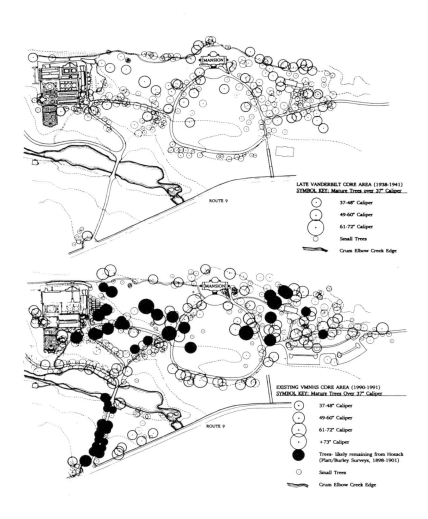

See citation 349. Patricia M. O'Donnell. "Cultural Landscape
Analysis: the Vanderbilt Estate at Hyde Park." *APT Bulletin*, 1992.
The historic periods of the core area of the landscape, 1938-41, and
1990-91, are shown with the individual tree collection, annotated by
size and implied age to show continuity.

Step-by-step methodology for park preservation: defining the client, assembling project team, delineating tasks and objectives. Role of landscape architect. Case study: Emerald Necklace Parks, Boston/Brookline, Mass. bib. illus.

352. O'Donnell, Patricia M. "The Rehabilitation of Red Creek Bridge: Genesee Valley Park, Rochester." *CRM* 16, no.4 (1993): pp.29-31.

Planning and treatment for one of four extant Olmsted Brothers designed bridges (1917). Part of park-wide master plan. Pre-construction testing, cleaning and substitute materials. bib. illus.

353. O'Donnell, Patricia M. "Relating Integrity to Interpretation." *CRM* 17, no.7 (1994): pp.12-15.

The relationship between the level of integrity of a landscape and the techniques for conveying its significance to the public through examples: Lyndhurst, Tarrytown, N.Y.; Vanderbilt Estate, Hyde Park, N.Y.; Ebey's Landing, Whidbey Island, Wash.; Cornelius Low House, New Brunswick, N.J. and St. Mary's City, Md. bib. illus.

354. O'Donnell, Patricia M. "The Treatment of Historic Landscapes." *Historic Preservation Forum* 7, no.3 (1993): pp.36-45.

Treatment selection, and application of the draft "Guidelines for the Treatment of Historic Landscapes." Case studies: Gettysburg National Military Park, Gettysburg, Pa.; Benjamin Franklin Parkway, Philadelphia, Pa., Monticello, Charlottesville, Va. bib. illus.

355. O'Donnell, Patricia M.; Melnick Robert Z. "Toward a Preservation Ethic." *Landscape Architecture* 77, no.4 (1987): p.136.

Editorial on the status of landscape preservation.

356. Oldham, Sally G. "Heritage Areas: A Policy Perspective" *The George Wright Forum* 8, no.2 (1991): pp.17-25.

See citation 352: Patricia M. O'Donnell. "The Rehabilitation of Red Creek Bridge: Genesee Valley Park, Rochester." *CRM*, 1993. Deterioration of deck, parapet wall and efflorescence (top) and finished view (bottom). Although some remnants of earlier stains are still visible, new construction blends with original.

Procedures for designation, formal justification. Dangers of competition between conservation/preservation and tourism, jurisdictional oversight, funding, discussed.

357. Oldham, Sally G. "Heritage Areas: A Policy Perspective." *Historic Preservation Forum* 6, no.2 (1992): pp.40-51.

History, definition, designation, justification and funding. Relevant legislation and policy. Education and outreach. Fit with natural, scenic, cultural and recreational resources.

358. Olmert, Michael. "In Seven-League Gum Boots, She Guards the Past." *Smithsonian* (1993): pp.121-127.

Quasi-governmental agency, Historic Buildings and Monuments Commission for England, also known as English Heritage, or EH, utilizes "field monument wardens" to perform on-going monitoring of historic buildings and landscapes (including ancient burial mounds, earthworks, Roman walls) under private ownership. illus.

359. Olmsted, Frederick Law. "Reforesting the Boston Harbor Islands: A Proposal [1887]" *Arnoldia* 48, no.3 (1988): pp.26-27.

Olmsted Sr.'s landscape treatment proposal offers historic perspective on preservation planning. Reprinted from "Thirteenth Annual Report of the Board of Commissioners for the Year 1887," Boston: Department of Parks, 1888.

360. O'Neill, Anthony and Barbara. "The Tourist's Landscape" *Landscape Design* no.202 (July/Aug.'91): pp.46-48.

Republic of Ireland planning Acts and the environment; establishing national park and archaeological sites; provisions for accommodating tourists while preserving historic and landscape features. illus.

361. Orlando, Cynthia; Luxenberg, Gretchen. "Ebey's Landing National Historical Reserve: Non-Traditional Management of a Nationally Significant Resource." *Trends* 29, no.2 (1992): pp.38-42.

Local participation in planning, managment, design guideline development and interpretation of 17,400 acre rural community. History, legislation enabling development of first U.S. Historical Reserve (1970's). illus.

362. Owen-John, Henry. "Archaeology and Agriculture: Some Current Issues." *Conservation Bulletin* 22, (1994): pp.18-20.

History of U.K. programs, Common Agricultural Policy and Set Aside scheme for agricultural lands. Ideas for partnerships between English Heritage and other government agencies and land owning/farming associations to establish the potential of archaeological return. bib. illus.

363. Paca, Barbara. "Management and Protection of Historic Eastern Hemlocks." *CRM* 16, no.4 (1993): pp.38-42.

History and impact of hemlock wooly adelgid (Adelges tsugae) predator. 'Lyndhurst,' 'Springside,' 'Sunnyside,' 'Sarah Lawrence cottage,' and the Mianus River Gorge Preserve discussed. bib. illus.

364. Paine, Cecelia. "Landscape Management of Abandoned Cemeteries in Ontario." *APT Bulletin* 24, no.3&4 (1992): pp.59-68.

Management, maintenance guidance for Ontario cemeteries under municipal jurisdiction. In Ontario, two thousand of five thousand cemeteries are abandoned. Emphasis on vegetation treatment, maintenance equipment use. bib. illus.

365. Paine, Cecelia. "Restoration of the Billings Estate Cemetery." *APT Bulletin* 15, no.4 (1983): pp.60-65.

Ottawa, Canada National Historic Site, occupied by Billings family from 1812-1975. City restores fences, vegetation, gravestones; documents process, future recommendations. bib. illus.

366. Pape, Alan C. "Preserving Cultural Landscapes." *Historic Preservation Forum* 5, no.1 (1991): pp.26-29.

Wisconsin Ethnic Corridor Project interprets German Old World influences on the landscape as part of state-wide cultural landscape preservation and tourism promotion project. illus.

367. Park Historic Architecture Division. "Earthworks Landscape Management Manual." Washington, D.C.: Park Historic Architecture Division, Cultural Resources, National Park Service, U.S. Department of the Interior, 1989.illus.

368. Parker, Patricia L., ed. "Traditional Cultural Properties:What You Do and How We Think." *CRM* 16, no.Special Issue (1993): 59 pp.

   Reflections three years after the publication of National Register Bulletin 38. Includes assessments and updates by program staff, outside professionals and communities. Research, documentation, inventory and analysis methodologies. illus.

369. Parkways: Past, Present, and Future: Proceedings of the Second Biennial Linear Parks Conference 1987., Boone, North Carolina, 1987. Boone, North Carolina: Appalachian Consortium Press, 1989. 336 pp.

   Forty-two papers addressing design and planning, historical perspectives, environmental and economic perspectives, and management. bib. illus.

370. Paterson, Douglas D.; Colby, Lisa J. "Heritage Landscapes in British Columbia: A guide to their identification, documentation and preservation." Vancouver, British Columbia: University of British Columbia, 1989. 66 pp.

   General guide to the identification, documentation, and preservation of British Columbia rural and vernacular landscapes. bib. illus.

371. Patten, Gerald D. "Cultural Landscapes: The Intent and the Tenor of the Times." *CRM* 14, no.6 (1991): pp. 1,3.

   Recognition for protecting a national legacy. Leadership goals: National Historic Landmark Theme Study; support local efforts, partnerships, development of guidelines, training and technological advances.

372. Patton, George E.; Menke, William F. "Design with Nature and Culture: The Long Meadow, Prospect Park, Brooklyn,

New York as Exemplar of an Urban Park Compatible with its Past." *Journal of Garden History* 2, no.4 (1982): pp.361-376.

Olmsted and Vaux design for nineteenth century park necessitates management respecting design intent, but adapted for modern use. bib. illus.

373. Penning, Rowsell Edmund. "Landscape Evaluation in Practice: A Survey of Local Authorities." *Landscape Research* 14, no.2 (1989): pp.35-37.

Survey of 165 U.K. public sector authorities regarding their use of landscape evaluation techniques. Of the 67% who responded, 22% report using such techniques. Need to support aesthetic judgements on landscape with stronger research base. bib. illus.

374. Phibbs, John. "An Approach to the Methodology of Recording Historic Landscapes." *Garden History* 2, no.2 (1983): pp.167-175.

Outline of kinds of site and archival surveys needed to make a clear presentation model, pointing out limitations inherent in these surveys and listing what the model should include. bib.

375. Phibbs, John. "A Reconsideration of Repton's Contribution to the Improvements at Felbrigg, Norfolk, 1778-84." *Garden History* 13, no.1 (1985): pp.33-44.

Advances the hypothesis that Repton did his first known 'proposed portrait' for the Felbrigg landscape under the influence of Nathaniel Kent. Example of inductive reasoning from existing evidence. illus.

376. Pick, Martin. "Aerial Photography." *The Garden Cities and Town Planning Magazine* 10, no.4 (1920): pp.71-87.

London magazine's post-World War I description of adaptation of aerial photography to town planning. Uses for large and small areas, equipment, comparison with survey maps described. illus.

377. Pitt, David G.; Phipps, Tim; Lessley, Billy V. "Participation in Maryland's Agricultural Land Preservation Program: The

Adoption of an Innovative Agricultural Land Policy."
Landscape Journal 7, no.1 (1988): pp.15-30.

Landowner participation in agricultural districting and
development rights acquisition programs of the Maryland
Agriculture Land Preservation Foundation. Data collection
through interviews. bib. illus.

378. Pitte, Jean Robert. "The Conservation of Parks and Gardens
in France." *Landscape Research* 12, no.2 (1987): pp.10-12.

Current role of municipalities. Case studies: Bagatelle,
Giverny, Les Alyscamps and Villandry, L'Isle-Adam and
Retz. illus.

379. Pollock-Ellwand, Nancy. "Heritage Advocacy in the Cultural
Landscape." *APT Bulletin* 24, no.3&4 (1992): pp.71-78.

Preservation planning, advocacy for 40,000 roadside trees in
Canadian rural township near Toronto. Inventory, planning
and protection strategies. bib. illus.

380. Porter, Jane. "Saving our Plant Heritage." *Landscape Design*
no.179 (Apr.'89): p.9.

National Council for the Conservation of Plants and Gardens
(NCCPG) dedicated to prevention of loss of plant varieties.

381. Potteiger, Matthew. "Preserving the Experience of
Landscape." *Landscape Architecture* 77, no.4 (1987):
pp.40-45.

Folklife expressions (e.g. songs, festivals, hunting, boat
building) shaping land patterns, spatial organizations and uses.
Case study: New Jersey Pine Barrens. bib. illus.

382. Potter, Elisabeth Walton; Boland, Beth M. *Guidelines for
Evaluating and Registering Cemeteries and Burial Places.*,
U.S. Department of the Interior. National Park Service
Cultural Resources. Interagency Resources Division.,
Washington, D.C., 33 pp.

American burial customs and cemeteries. Descriptions and
types of burial places and their associated features. Guidance
for successful preparation of nominations. Mapping, field

I

TREE INVENTORY-METHOD

1.   Locate fixed point at the centre of the intersection of two roads.
     Assign this point a letter. (A, A', B, B', C...) A for north side A' for south side.

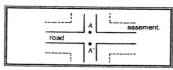

2.   Measure and record the distance from the centre line of the road to the edge of the road easement. (b) Write this, in metres, in the distance column of the inventory sheet.

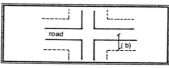

3.   Measure from the centre line of the road to the first tree that has a minimum diameter of 35 cm.
     Record the tree number and the distance in the appropriate columns on the
     "Tree Inventory" sheet.

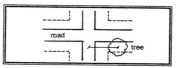

4.   Measure and record, in the DBH column, the diameter of the trunk 1.3 m above the ground; using a diameter tape and recording in cm.

5.   Identify and record the tree species, crown vigour (using the 1-5 scale) and note the presence of any problems listed on the inventory sheet. The attached glossary will provide further detail of the categories.

6.   Record, in the appropriate column, the land use and type of fence adjacent to the tree. Categories are listed in the glossary.

7.   In the notes column identify the location and size of hydro lines, the status of ditches and any other pertinent information, not covered by the other categories.
     For example: heart rot, tree in decline, land owner, heritage home, part of a woodlot, new plantings near by, etcetera.

8.   Measure, cumulative from the start point, to the second tree of 35 cm diameter or greater. Record the distance , and repeat steps 3 -7.

9.   Begin the " Tree Formations" and " General Roadside Characteristics " sheets.

Notes : Record only the trees with a minimum diameter of 35 cm at breast height(approx.1.3 m)
     : All distance measures must be cumulative from the fixed point.
     : UTM locator co-ordinates are to be established at home base using appropriate calculations

See citation 379: Nancy Pollack-Ellwand. "Heritage Advocacy in the Landscape." *APT Bulletin*, 1992. Excerpt from Roadside Tree Inventory Manual, 1992, created to instruct volunteers collecting information on roadside trees.

work, archaeology, photography, setting boundaries,
documentation and assessment techniques. Step-by-step
process for determining integrity and significance. bib. illus.

383. Proceedings of the Canadian Parks Service Reconstruction
Workshop., Hull, Quebec, 11-13 March 1992. Canada:
National Historic Sites, Parks Service, Environment Canada,
1993. 107 pp.

   Proceedings addressing five issues including: Challenges the
CPS Faces with Existing Reconstructions; Values of
Reconstructions as They Relate to Presentation; What CPS
Should Do with its Ageing Reconstructions; Alternatives to
Period Reconstruction; and Criteria for Reconstructions in the
Future.

384. Proceedings of the First International Symposium on
Protection and Restoration of Historical Gardens.,
Fountainebleu, France, 13-18 September 1971. Paris, France:
ICOMOS, 1971. 250 pp.

   First international symposium on the preservation of historic
parks and gardens. English language papers include: Special
Problems Connected with the Conservation of Gardens of
Historical Interest in Japan, Mitsuo Yokoyama; Special
Problems Connected with the Conservation of Gardens of
Historical Interest in Czechoslovakia, Olga Baseova; Special
Problems Connected with the Conservation of Gardens of
Historical Interest in Great Britain, Laurence Fricker;
'Historical Gardens in Hungary, Karoly Orsi; Closing Speech
by the President of ICOMOS, Piero Gazzola. Future
recommendations, participant list, schedule. illus.

385. Pulsipher, Lydia Mihelic. "They Have Saturdays and Sundays
to Feed Themselves." *Expedition (The University Museum
Magazine of Archaeology and Anthropology, University of
Pennsylvania)* 32, no.2 (1990): pp.24-33.

   Historical documents, in-situ landscape analysis, oral history
and current cultivation practices used to identify and describe
three types of Caribbean slave gardens on Galways plantation,
Island of Monserrat. bib. illus.

386. Purcell, Donovan. "The Repair and Preservation of Stonework." *Garden History Society: Occasional Paper #1* (1969): pp.11-14.

     Excluding water-carrying salts is most effective way to protect outdoor stonework; need to determine cause of damage before starting repair; types of stone, use of artificial stone discussed.

387. Rabinowitz, Richard. "Interpreting in the Landscape: A Herbridean Perspective." *CRM* 17, no.7 (1994): pp.10-11, 47.

     Three approaches from an interpreter's perspective: interpretation placed on, carried into, and built out of the resource. National examples. bib. illus.

388. Rafkind, Chuck; Devine, Hugh; Karish, John F.; Dienna, Patti. "What We've Learned About GIS: One Park's Experience in the World of Geographic Information Systems." *The George Wright Forum* 10, no.3 (1993): pp.30-37.

     Case study at Colonial National Historic Park, Yorktown, Va. Twelve information layers comprise GIS system, including fire history, exotic and noxious vegetation species, National Registerr of Historic Places, soils, etc. Database management, hardware, software capabilities, costs, discussed.

389. Raikes, Gill. "An Enterprising Spirit" *Landscape Design* no.206 (Dec.'91/Jan.'92): pp.39-41.

     National Trust's U.K. efforts to preserve the coastline. Representing traditional landscapes, agricultural practices, and settlements, preservation strategies are maintaining threatened segments of the U.K.'s historic coast. illus.

390. Ramsay, Juliet. *How to Record the National Estate Values of Gardens.*, Australian Government Publishing Service, Canberra, Australia, 1991. 24 pp.

     A guide to identifying, surveying and evaluating condition and integrity of a garden as required by the Commission. Step-by-step process for researching its history, compiling a written narrative and generating plan. Summary of the Australian Heritage Commission Criteria, examples of survey forms and garden layout plans. bib. illus.

391. Ramsay, Juliet. *Parks, Gardens and Special Trees: A Classification and assessment Method for the Register of the National Estate.*, Australian Government Publishing Service, Canberra, Australia, 1991. 54 pp.

To standardize the assessment of nominations, different category classifications are described. To establish common terminology, groups of gardens with similar characteristics, called "types" or "type profiles" are defined with representative examples. Two sections: classification methods; assessment process. Matrix, plans. bib. illus.

394. Rath, Frederick L. ,. Jr. "Oral History: The Hyde Park Project." *CRM* 16, no.10 (1993): pp.1,3-7,12.

George Palmer conducts National Park Service's first oral history project at Roosevelt-Vanderbilt National Historic Site, Hyde Park, N.Y. in 1947. Chronology, description of oral history as interpretive tool. illus.

395. "Recent Discussions and Publications." *Garden History* 3, no.4 (1975): pp.25-26.

Listing of thirty, mostly european garden preservation resources published between 1963 and 1975.

396. Reid, Debra Ann. "Open-Air Museums and Historic Sites." *APT Bulletin* 21, no.2 (1989): pp.21-27.

Results of 1986 survey of 138 U.S. historic sites, open-air museums, discussing research methodology, buffer zones, site development, interpretation. bib. illus.

397. Rempel, Sharon. "Conserving and Managing Living Plant Collections." *APT Bulletin* 24, no.3&4 (1992): pp.69-70.

Twenty-one questions as an aid for managers developing living plant collections policy. Annotated list of plant conservation organizations. bib.

398. "Report of Working Groups: Historic Transportation Corridors Conference." *CRM* 16, no.11 (1993): pp.54-55.

Outgrowth of 1992 San Antonio, Tex., conference. Definitions, characteristics, preservation planning, treatment and management. Application of World Heritage Criteria.

399. Rice, Barbara; MacNally, Marcia J. "The Bay Area Ridge Trail Council: A Model in Community Participation." *Trends* 29, no.2 (1992): pp.18-22.

Overview of proposed 400-mile, ten county ridgeline trail (including San Francisco), seventy-five parks and thirty open space juridsictions. Planning, management for national, scenic, cultural and historic resources. Partnership structure as a regional-scale example. illus.

400. Richardson, Bill. "Quaker Burial Grounds: Plainness Texts from Community and Family in Dutchess County, New York." *Material Culture* 25, no.1 (1993): pp.37-49.

Study of Quaker tombstones and discussion of tombstones as indicators of material culture. bib.

401. Rikard, Stephen. "An Integrated Approach" *Landscape Design* no.178 (Mar.'89): pp.28-33.

Travis Morgan Landscape Ltd., landscape architecture firm, has specialty in historic landscape project work. Performed historical survey, and is executing ten year Restoration Plan of Chiswick House Grounds, London. illus.

402. Risk, Paul. "Interpretation: A Road to Creative Enlightenment." *CRM* 16, no.11 (1993): pp.47-49.

Rationale, relationship to treatment and management; issues in interpreting corridors: length, continuity, absence of theme development, wayside stations, audio/visual tools, visitor centers, and more. bib.

403. Roberts, Frederick E. "Some Thoughts on Managing the Buffer." *The Public Garden* 3, no.2 (1988): pp.32-34.

Land management techniques to improve functional and aesthetic quality of historic and other gardens. illus.

404. Roberts, John M. "Visual Landscape Mapping and Computation." *APT Bulletin* 11, no.4 (1979): pp.88-100.

Author states that visual assessment parallels environmental assessment procedures required by the U.S. National Environmental Protection Act of 1970. Discusses on-site observation and programmable hand-held calculator for determining viewsheds. bib. illus.

405. Robinson, Eric. "Messages in Stone in God's Acre" *Landscape Design* no. 184 (Oct.'89): pp.38-40.

Urban cemeteries in the U.K. studied for weathering patterns on various types of stone used for monuments. bib. illus.

406. Robinson, Fred J. "Management and Treatment of Historic Views and Vistas: Stan Wyet Hall, Akron." *CRM* 16, no.4 (1993): pp.35-37.

Detailed vista restoration project at Tudor Revival estate designed by Warren H. Manning between 1911-15. illus.

407. Rogers, Elizabeth Barlow. "Rebuilding Central Park: A Management and Restoration Plan." Cambridge, Massachusetts and London, U.K.: MIT Press, 1987. 160 pp.

Preservation planning for N.Y.C., N.Y. landmark. Historic overview and detailed methodology for park analysis and later management. Divides park into twenty-two project areas, each with plans and photographs. Overview of Central Park Conservancy. illus.

408. Sales, John. "The Philosophy and Practice of Garden Preservation." *APT Bulletin* 17, no.3&4 (1985): pp.61-64.

Addresses maintenance, change and garden design evolving over time; U.K. garden history. Stourhead, Hidcote, Sissinghurst, Mottisfont, Powis Castele, Welshpool discussed.

409. Sales, John. "The Role of the National Trust in Garden Conservation and Restoration." *Garden History* 3, no.4 (1975): pp.50-61.

National Trust's U.K. holdings described; Trust's philosophy for private garden preservation compared to public parks or museums. illus.

410. Sanchez, Mario. "A Land Between Two Nations." *Historic Preservation Forum* 7, no.1 (1993): pp.36-41.

   Los Caminos de Rio is a project which interprets influences of two cultures on a two hundred mile river corridor to promote cultural tourism and cultural heritage and preservation. illus.

411. Sanchis, Frank. "Landscape Initiatives of the National Trust." *Historic Preservation Forum* 7, no.3 (1993): pp.62-65.

   New directions in stewardship. illus.

412. Savage, Beth L. "Listed in the National Register of Historic Places." *CRM* 16, no.11 (1993): pp.28-30.

   Overview of 61,000 listings as integral elements of larger transportation corridors. Definition, evaluation/nomination and relevant themes. Canals, military, wagon roads, railroads, parkways, highways discussed. illus.

413. Sawyers, Claire. "Mt. Cuba: Implementing a Policy." *The Public Garden* 1, no.3 (1986): pp.15-16.

   Development of native plant collection on historic twentieth century Greenville, Del., estate. illus.

414. Schmidt, Ray. "Interpreting Images: A Slice at a Time." *APT Bulletin* 15, no.4 (1983): pp.57-59.

   Work of Canadian Centres for Remote Sensing. Computerized aerial photographic images detect heat, decipher obscure patterns. LANDSAT, density slicers, digitized images. illus.

415. Seager, Pamela. "Treading Softly." *The Public Garden* 7, no.2 (1992): pp.18-20,38.

   Preservation planning, treatment, interpretation and management for Ranchos Los Alamitos, Long Beach, Calif., dealing with change at the Bixby family property, 1868 to present. Issues include geographic context, reduction in site (from 300,000 to 7.5 acres), public access, universal design. Long term treatment proposals. illus.

See citation 415: Pamela Seager. "Treading Softly." *The Public Garden*, 1992. The treatment of the Jacaranda Walk is part of the Rancho Los Alamitos Preservation Master Plan, Long Beach, Calif. Paired views of 1936 and 1992 photos.

416. Second International Symposium on Protection and Restoration
of Historical Gardens, Organized by ICOMOS and IFLA.,
Granada, Spain, 29 October & 4 November 1973. Paris,
France: ICOMOS, 1975. 282 pp.

Second international symposium on garden and park
preservation. English language papers include: 'Islamic
Gardens in Iran,' Mr. Daneshboust; 'Anatolian Turkish
Gardens,' Mrs. Gonul Aslanoglu Evyapan; 'Problems of
Garden Archeology in the U.S.S.R.,' Mrs. Micoulina and
Mrs. Tochtahojaeva; 'The Gardens of Egypt,' Mr. Mohammad
Hammad; 'The Muslim Gardens of the Arabian Peninsula,'
Mr. Mohammed Hammad; 'Gardens of India,' Mr. Prabhakar
B. Bhagwat; 'On the Origin of the Patios and Gardens of the
Islamic Period in Spain and Portugal,' Mr. Ilidio A.
DeAraujo. All foreign language papers inlude english language
summary. 'Closing Address by the President of ICOMOS,'
Piero Gazzola. Recommendations, participant list and
schedule. illus.

417. *Secretary of the Interior's Standards for the Treatment of
Historic Properties.*, U.S. Department of the Interior. National
Park Service. Cultural Resources. Preservation Assistance.,
Washington, D.C., rev., 1992. Brochure.

History and purpose of program. Definitions and standards
for four primary treatments: preservation, rehabilitation,
restoration and reconstruction. illus.

418. Shapovalova, Elena F. "Gostilitsy: A Country Estate in
Russia." *Landscape Design* no.199 (Apr.'91): pp.42-45.

Eighteenth and nineteenth century history of site grounds.
Description of modifications, adjacent housing project's impact
on historic landscape. illus.

419. Shaw, Jonathan A. "Every Tree Doomed: The Reforestation
of Harvard Yard." *Harvard Magazine* 96, no.6 (1994):
pp.46-53.

Strategy for replacing American Elm (Ulmus americana).
Canopy, branching structure, species diversity, seasonal
interest, micro-climate, disease resistance, foundation

plantings, soil compaction, management, maintenance discussed. illus.

420. Shepheard, Peter Sir. "The Rewards of Restoration" *Landscape Design* no.193 (Sept.'90): pp.14-17.

Restoration of Charleston Farmhouse Gardens, Sussex, U.K. to the period of the 1930's outlined. illus.

421. Sherwood, Mary P. "Renaissance at Walden." *Arnoldia* 46, no.3 (1986): pp.47-58.

History of Walden Pond rehabilitation through revegetation. illus.

422. Shupe, Brian. "The Mad River Valley Initiative." *Historic Preservation Forum* 5, no.3 (1991): pp.38-43.

Mad River area in Vt. organized as a local certified government and initiated planning efforts to preserve and protect local landscapes from unmanaged growth.

423. Sicca, Cinzia Maria, compiler. "Current Bibliography of Garden History." *Journal of Garden History* 6, no.1 (1986): pp.62-84.

Includes publications from British National Bibliography, Art Index, Repertoire d'art et d'archeologie, RICA, and other periodicals; in fifteen categories. bib., annotated.

424. Sinha, Amita. "The Conservation of Sacred Sites: Sarnath, a case study." *Landscape Research* 16, no.3 (1991): pp.23-30.

Sarnath, in northern India, said to have been the Buddha's first sermon site: research issues, environmental qualities of Indian and other sacred spaces, treatment of ruins, protection of natural areas. bib. illus.

425. Sisa, Jozsef; Orsi, Karoly. "Conserving Historic Parks and Gardens in Hungary." *Landscape Research* 12, no.2 (1987): pp.22-26.

Role of the National Commission of Historic Buildings, founded in 1957. No Renaissance gardens in Hungary survive. Eighteenth and nineteenth century case studies described: Alcsut, Sereglelyes, Nagycenk, Eger. bib. illus.

426. Skinner, Helen Ross. "With a Lilac by the Door." *APT Bulletin* 15, no.4 (1983): pp.35-37.

Dirth of primary documentary references for dates of introduction of common plants such as lilacs, day lillies in early Ontario gardens. Island beds popular, flowering shrubs planted along fence lines, vegetable gardens more important than flower gardens. bib.

427. Smith, Samuel D. "Site Survey as a Method for Determining Historic Site Significance." *Historical Archaeology* 24, no.2 (1990): pp.34-41.

Tennessee Division of Archaeology's four site survey methodologies explore National Register Criterion (d), the 'information value of sites:' thematic site surveys (ex. frontier stations); representative county surveys; cultural resource surveys; state owned area surveys. bib. illus.

428. Sniderman, Julia. "Project Work in Chicago's Historic Parks." *CRM* 16, no.4 (1993): pp.10-13.

Comprehensive basis for managing city-wide system of park resources. Methodologies for inventory, integrity evaluation, registration, nomination and treatment. Grant Park case study. illus.

429. Sniderman, Julia; Nathan, Jo Ann. "Reawakening a Spirit of Stewardship." *Landscape Architecture* 77, no.5 (1987): pp.88-93.

Preservation planning, legislation, design guidelines for the treatment of planned community of Highland Park, Lakeside, Ill., (Cleveland and French, 1869). Role of Highland Park Historic Preservation Commission. Highland Park sites discussed: Rosewood Park (Rosenwald estate, designed by Jens Jensen), Ravinia Station. bib. illus.

430. Snyder, John W. "Historic Preservation and Hazardous Waste: A Legacy of the Industrial Past." *APT Bulletin* 24, no.1&2 (1992): pp.67-73.

Hazardous waste abatement at historic non-process industrial sites, such as railroads; potential re-use; list of historic processes and materials in daily operation of Southern Pacific Railroad sites in Sacramento and Oakland Calif. bib. illus.

431. Spennemann, Dirk H. R. "Multicultural Resources Management." *Historic Preservation Forum* 7, no.1 (1993): pp.20-26.

A multi-cultural heritage management approach does not necessarily represent all cultural entities and therefore skews heritage interpretation. Examples include Pacific cultures. illus.

432. Spongberg, Stephen A.; Del Tredici, Peter. "Historic Plants in a New Setting: The Evolution of the Hunnewell Building Landscape." *Arnoldia* 53, no.4 (1993-94): pp.20-25.

Rehabilitation of visitor center landscape at the Arnold Arboretum, Jamaica Plain, Mass., as an interpretation of history of the Arboretum. illus.

433. Starke, Barry M. *Maymont Park--The Italian Garden.*, National Park Service, Washington, D.C., 1980.

Rehabilitation plan for historic Richmond, Va. garden. Plans, sections, specifications and details with an emphasis on masonry. bib. illus.

434. Stewart, John J. "Debating Scrape Versus Anti-scrape in the Gardens at Bellevue Terrace." *APT Bulletin* 18, no.1&2 (1986): pp.43-46.

Determination of appropriate levels of intervention in historic landscape treatment, particularly with vegetation. Case study: 1841 home and garden of Canada's first Prime Minister, Sir John Macdonald, Bellevue House National Historic Site, Kingston, Ontario. illus.

435. Stewart, John J. "Incorporating Photographs into Working Drawings." *APT Bulletin* 9, no.3 (1977): pp.21-29.

Integrating historic visual documentation into treatment documents. illus.

436. Stewart, John J. "Landscape Archeology: Existing Plant Material on Historic Sites as Evidence of Buried Features and as Survivors of Existing Species." *APT Bulletin* 9, no.3 (1977): pp.65-72.

Low-level archaeology investigation alternatives. illus.

437. Stewart, John J. "Landscape Archeologist at Work: How to 'Do Archaeology' Without Really Digging." *Landscape Architecture* 68, no.2 (1978): pp.140-144.

Non-excavational techniques for researching historic landscapes. illus.

438. Stewart, John J.; Buggey, Susan. "The Case for Commemoration of Historic Landscapes and Gardens." *APT Bulletin* 7, no.2 (1975): pp.99-123.

For each of six criteria for historic landscapes and gardens, several Canadian examples are given. Criteria based upon 1971 Historic Garden Symposium's joint committee of the International Council on Monuments and Sites (ICOMOS) and the International Federation of Landscape Architects (IFLA), held at Fontainebleau. bib. illus.

439. Stipe, Robert E.; Lee, Antoinette J., eds. "The American Mosaic: Preserving a Nation's Heritage." Washington, D.C.: US/ICOMOS, United States Committee International Council on Monuments and Sites, 1987.

Essays include: Historic Preservation : The Process and the Actors, Robert E. Stipe; The Federal Government as Standard Bearer, John M. Fowler; The States: Preservation in the Middle, Elizabeth A. Lyon; Where the Action Is: Preservation and Local Governments, J. Myrick Howard; What Do We Preserve and Why? W. Brown Morton, III; Discovering the Old Cultures in the New World: The Role of Ethnicity, Antoinette J. Lee; Historic Preservation in the Private Sector, Gregory E. Andrews; Beneath the American Mosaic: The Place of Archaeology, Thomas F. King; The Next 20 Years, Robert E. Stipe. illus.

440. Stokes, Samuel N.; Watson, A. Elizabeth; Keller, Genevieve P.; Keller, J. Timothy. "Saving Americas Countryside: A

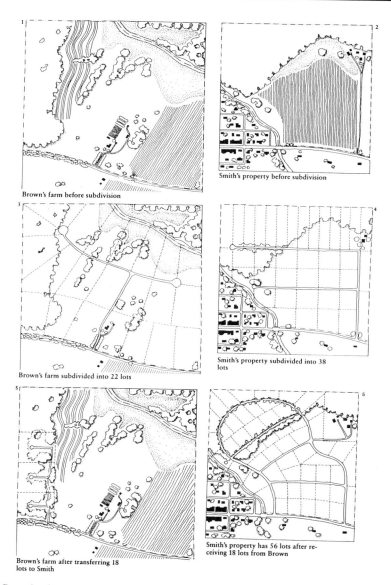

Brown's farm before subdivision

Smith's property before subdivision

Brown's farm subdivided into 22 lots

Smith's property subdivided into 38 lots

Brown's farm after transferring 18 lots to Smith

Smith's property has 56 lots after receiving 18 lots from Brown

See citation 440. Samuel N. Stokes, A. Elizabeth Watson, Genevieve P. Keller, and J. Timothy Keller. *Saving Americas Countryside: A Guide to Rural Conservation*. 1989. Sample case study of the transfer of development rights (TDR) from the Brown farm to the Smith property.

Guide to Rural Conservation." Baltimore, Maryland: National
Trust for Historic Preservation and Johns Hopkins University
Press, 1989. 306 pp.

Present day concerns and trends. Strategies and tools for
identifying, analyzing, preserving and protecting rural and
vernacular landscapes. National case studies include
conservation programs, land protection techniques, voluntary
tecnhiques for protecting private property and community
outreach and education. Sources of assistance and suggested
readings. bib., annotated. illus.

441. Stone, Gaynell. "Material Evidence of Idealogical and Ethnic
Choice in Long Island Gravestones, 1670-1820." *Material
Culture* 23, no.3 (1991): pp.1-29.

Study findings indicate ethnic and cultural settlement
patterns. bib. illus.

442. Strangstad, Lynette. "A Graveyard Preservation Primer." 2d
ed. Nashville, Tennessee: American Association for State and
Local History, 1990.

A "how-to" manual. Inventory, data collection, archaeology,
and assessment strategies. Organizational concerns: rubbings,
volunteer coordination, public awareness, security,
interpretation and funding. Sample survey forms. bib.,
annotated. illus.

443. Strangstad, Lynette. *Preservation of Historic Burial Grounds.*,
National Trust for Historic Preservation, Washington, D.C.,
1994. 24 pp.

Preservation planning guide. Project organization, necessary
professionals, archaeology, maintenance, management,
treatment and phasing. Cleaning burial markers. Preserving
historic plant materials (by Scott Kunst). Case studies: Mt.
Moriah Cemetery, Deadwood, N. Dak.; Magnolia Cemetery,
Mobile, Ala.; and Randolph Cemetery, Columbia, S.C.
Sample survey sheet for individual grave markers. Other
national examples. bib. illus.

444. Streatfield, David C. "Preservation of a California Oasis: Rancho Los Alamitos, Long Beach." *CRM* 16, no.4 (1993): pp.23-25.

   Preservation issues regarding a ranch that shrank from 300,000 acres (1790) to 7 1/2 acres (1970's). Application of draft 'Guidelines for the Treatment of Historic Landscapes.' Evaluation of visual relationships between the gardens and geographic context. bib. illus.

445. Streatfield, David C. "Standards for Historic Garden Preservation and Restoration." *Landscape Architecture* 66, no.3 (1969): pp.198-204.

   Historic perspective of landscape preservation philosophy and the need for a national approach. Focus on designed landscapes. Case studies. illus.

446. Striner, Richard. *Preservation and the Recent Past.*, National Trust for Historic Preservation, Washington, D.C., 1994. 24 pp.

   Overview of issues and strategies. Case study format with focus on resources whose significance relates to twentieth century history including motor resources (e.g. shopping centers, parkways) and post-World War II resources. Emphasis on structures. National examples. bib. illus.

447. Sykes, Meredith; Stewart, John J. "Historic Landscape Restoration in the United States and Canada: An Annotated Source Outline." *APT Bulletin* 4, no.3&4 (1972): pp.114-158.

   Annotated bibliographic references to historic gardens in the U.S. and Canada dating from the seventeenth to the twentieth centuries. Each reference has description of several paragraphs; approximately thirty references listed on restored gardens, historical references, archaeology, seed sources. bib., annotated. illus.

448. "Symposium: The Treatment of the Surroundings of Historic Buildings." *Garden History* 3, no.4 (1975): pp.22-24.

   Report from 1975 Garden History Society Heritage Year Symposium, held in London. Clause 12, Town and Country Amenities Act, providing for grants to historic gardens discussed; also a clause stating that public opinion must be tested on preservation planning actions "which may be detrimental to a building's setting."

449. Tagger, Barbara. "Corridors as Cultural Landscapes: Selma to Montgomery National Trail." *CRM* 16, no.11 (1993): pp.34-35.

   Historic background, eligibility criteria and evaluation of trail and potential routes. Public outreach and implementation strategies.

450. Tamulevich, Susan. "New Science for Old Gardens." *Mid-Atlantic Country* no.15 (1994): 5. pp. 30-37, 89, 96-98.

   Evolution of historic landscape restoration demonstrated through four case studies: Historic Bartram's Garden, Philadelphia, Pa.; Old Salem, Winston-Salem, N.C.; Pompeii in Rome; William Paca House garden, Annapolis, Md. illus.

451. Taylor, Ken. "Historical Cultural Landscapes and Emerging Heritage Values: An Australian Perspective." *Landscape Research* 15, no.2 (1990): pp.12-18.

   Historic overview, emerging awareness of cultural landscapes. National strategies, public and private initiatives, Australian ICOMOS framework as preservation planning tool. Case study: Lanyon-Lambrigg rural landscape. bib. illus.

452. Taylor, Ken. "Interpretative Values and Cultural Landscapes: An Australian Perspective." *CRM* 17, no.7 (1994): pp.16-18.

   Developments post-1970: assessing significance, recognition of social history. Influence of Australia ICOMOS Charter for the Conservation of Places of Cultural Significance (The Burra Charter) on practice. Examples: Lonyon Homestead, Canberra; and, Port Arthur Penitentiary. bib. illus.

453. *Technologies for Prehistoric and Historic Preservation.*, U.S. Congress, Office of Technology Assessment, Washington, D.C., 1986. 186 pp.

   Background and summary of findings: preservation process, treatment issues, applied technology, public information, and federal policy. Landscape and archaeology discussed. illus.

454. *Technologies for the Preservation of Prehistoric and Historic Landscapes--Background Paper.*, U.S. Congress, Office of Technology Assessment, Washington, D.C., 1987. 46 pp.

Technology and legislative recommendations pertaining to: landscape identification, the need for a center for preservation technology, and federal policy. bib. illus.

455. Third International Symposium on Protection and Restoration of Historical Gardens, Organized by ICOMOS and IFLA., Zeist, Netherlands, 8-13 September 1975. Paris, France: ICOMOS, 1975. 231 pp.

Third international symposium on historic gardens. English language papers include: 'From the Historic to the Total Garden: Some Considerations Based on the Cultural and Related Influences of Botanic and Other Gardens of the Past,' Frans Verdoorn; 'Ornamental Plants in 16th and 17th Century Gardens. An annotated list...,' C.S. Oldenburger-Ebbers and J. Heniger; 'For the Historic Gardens and Parts of the Netherlands, the Danger-Signal is Alight,' Mr. Kamerlingh-Ohnes; 'Notes....,' Halian National Committee,' Desidena Pasolini; 'Historical Gardens in the Federal Republic of Germany: Risks and Experiences,' Miss Gerda Gollwitzer; 'Historic Garden Preservation in the United States: Its History and Present State,' Dr. Elisabeth B. MacDougall. Several articles on Dutch gardens to supplement field visits, participants list and schedule. illus.

456. Thomas, Graham S. "The Restoration of Gardens with Special Reference to the National Trust." *Garden History Society:Occasional Paper #1* (1969): pp.7-10.

General description of National Trust's U.K. garden restoration efforts regarding vegetation renewal, species selection, maintenance, personnel.

457. Tishler, William H. "The Landscape: An Emerging Historic Preservation Resource." *APT Bulletin* 11, no.4 (1979): pp.9-25.

Author regrets still limited recognition of the role of landscape in federal historic preservation progams in the U.S. and Canada; commends the Canadian National Heritage

Program of the Heritage Conservation and Recreation Service. bib. illus.

458. Tishler, William H.; Buggey, Susan, ed. Alliance for Landscape Preservation: Proceedings from the Clearing and Williamsburg., The Clearing, Door County, Wisconsin and Colonial Williamsburg, Williamsburg, Virginia, 1979 and 1980. Madison, Wisconsin: Department of Landscape Architecture, University of Wisconsin, Madison, 1983. 112 pp. bib. illus.

459. Tomlan, Michael. "Historic Preservation Education: Alongside Architecture in Academia." *Journal of Architectural Education* 47, no.4 (1994): pp.187-196.

Development of higher education preservation curricula; recommendations for coordinating, integrating, architectural and preservation education programs. bib.

460. Toole, R. M. "Historic Landscape Architecture on the Hudson River Valley Estates." *APT Bulletin* 15, no.4 (1983): pp.39-40.

Case study in documentation of mid-nineteenth century estate grounds, built during the time of Andrew Jackson Downing. Hudson River Shorelands Task Force performs inventory and evaluation, uses aerial photography, oral history, etc. Need to recognize the landscape as part of historic resource.

461. Toth, Edward. *An Ecosystem Approach to Woodland Management: The Case of Prospect Park.*, National Association for Olmsted Parks, Bethesda, Maryland, 1991. 14 pp.

Urban park management for 1866 Olmsted/Vaux designed historic park. Over 100 acres of remnant woodland in various states of deterioration are addressed by specialized maintenance crews for horticulture, lawns, and natural resources. Six main tasks: controlling slope erosion, arresting soil depletion, controlling invasive species, replanting interior gaps, understory restoration and minimizing disturbance. Ravine I case study. Management zones and associated plant lists. Plans. bib. illus.

462. Travis, Tara. "Canyon de Chelly National Monument: Interpreting a Dynamic Cultural System." *CRM* 17, no.7 (1994): pp.19-22.

     Increasing visitor understanding through cultural landscape study. History of evolution and occupation of Arizona Canyon. Current studies inform interpretive and preservation planning decisions. bib. illus.

463. Treib, Marc. "The Care and Feeding of the Noble Allee." *Arnoldia* 54, no.1 (1994): pp.12-23.

     History, preservation of allees and bosks at the Tuileries and Sceaux. Species selection, contemporary management, maintenance. illus.

464. Triantafillou, Menelaos and Eric. "Historic Landscape Reconstruction." *Landscape Architecture* 83, no.6 (1993): pp.82-83.

     Computer-generated visual simulation as a visual reconstruction tool. Overview of process: data input, image editing, output storage and results. Case study: Temple of Zeus at the Acropolis, Athens, Greece. illus.

465. Triantafillou, Menelaos. "Visual Simulation as a Tool for Interpretation." *CRM* 17, no.7 (1994): pp.35-37.

     Computerized visual reconstructions to depict a landscape during significant periods of its development as an alternative to physical reconstruction. Case studies: Temple of Zeus, at the Acropolis, Athens, Greece; Elmhurst Estate, Perintown, Ohio (unexecuted design by Gertrude Jekyll). bib. illus.

466. Tromp, Heimerick. "The Park of Het Huys ten Donck, near Ridderkerk: An Example of Historical Research on Behalf of the Protection of Country Seats in The Netherlands." *Journal of Garden History* 1, no.4 (1981): pp.353-366.

     Survey of primary and secondary source materials. bib. illus.

467. Tucker, Arthur O. "Delmara: A Wasteland or Unexplored Wilderness of Horticulture?" *Magnolia* 8, no.3 (1992): pp.4-6.

Discussion of Delmara Peninsula, encompassing Del., Md., Va., as largely unexplored historical horticultural resource with designed and vernacular gardens and sites of former nurseries needing documentation. illus.

468. Turner, Richard G. ,. Jr. "The Experience of the Ruth Bancroft Garden and the Garden Conservancy." *The Public Garden* 8, no.1 (1993): pp.22-24.

Preservation efforts for Walnut Creek, Calif., garden which inspired the Garden Conservancy to preserve significant private gardens. illus.

469. Turner, Suzanne Louise. "Faithful to the Text." *Landscape Architecture* 77, no.4 (1987): pp.72-75.

Post-1970's approach to plantation landscapes; new rigor in research; opportunities for interpretation. Case studies: Hermann-Grima Historic House courtyard and Magnolia Mound Plantation, New Orleans, La. illus.

470. Turner, Suzanne Louise. "Historic Landscapes., in "American Landscape Architecture: Designers and Places." Tishler, William H., ed." Washington, D.C.: National Trust for Historic Preservation, the American Society of Landscape Architects and The Preservation Press, 1989. pp. 142-145.

Historic perspective and current practice. bib. illus.

471. Turner, Suzanne Louise. "Plantation Papers as a Source for Landscape Documentation and Interpretation: The Thomas Butler Papers." *APT Bulletin* 7, no.3 (1980): pp.28-45.

Department of Archives and Manuscripts, Louisiana State University, houses over ten thousand items from the Butler's Plantation, West Feliciana Parish, La., from 1768-1950. Archives studied for attitudes towards landscape, gardens, and for specific horticultural practices. Findings. bib. illus.

472. Turner, Suzanne Louise. "Time Goes On: Of Sugar Cane, Soybeans and Standard Oil." *Courier* 34, no.8 (1989): pp.6-9.

Landscape analysis, interpretation media. Example: southern Louisiana vernacular landscapes. illus.

See citation 474: UNESCO; David Harmon, ed. "Dubrovnik's Old City: The Destruction of a Heritage Cultural Site." *The George Wright Forum*, 1994. Diagram of Dubrovnik's Old City. Each black dot represents a direct hit by artillery from 1992 civil war. Solid black sections represent totally gutted buildings. (Adapted from an illustration by the Institute for the Protection of the Cultural Monuments and Natural Environment of Dubrovnik.)

473. Turner, Tom. "Parks Policy" *Landscape Design* no.216 (Dec.'92): pp.19-20.

Changes in use, management, and finance threaten British urban parks created between 1830 and 1930. Recommended actions.

474. UNESCO; Harmon, David, ed. "Dubrovnik's Old City: The Destruction of a Heritage Cultural Site." *The George Wright Forum* 11, no.1 (1994): pp.11-21.

Declared a World Heritage Site in 1979, during recent civil war, 68% of Old City buildings damaged. International preservation community response to disaster. illus.

475. Valen, Walden. "Strybing: Rebuilding an Established Collection." *The Public Garden* 1, no.3 (1986): pp.13-14.

Collections policy, master plan to rebuild Strybing Botanical Gardens, San Francisco, Calif. illus.

476. Van Valkenburgh, Michael; Del Tredici, Peter. "Restoring the Harvard Yard Landscape." *Arnoldia* 54, no.1 (1994): pp.2-11.

Current rehabilitation of tree canopy. List of recommended trees. Photographs, plan. illus.

477. Veloz, Nicolas F. "Outdoor Sculpture in the Park Environment." *CRM* 7, no.2 (1984): pp.4-7.

Case studies on two statues in D.C. National Parks. Cleaning and protective treatments. illus.

478. Veloz, Nicolas F.; Chase, W. Thomas. "Airbrasive Cleaning of Statuary and Other Structures: A Century of Technical Examination of Blasting Procedures." *Technology and Conservation* 10, no.1 (1989): pp.18-28.

Treatment alternatives that will not threaten resource. Technical. Source list. illus.

479. Vernon, Noel Dorsey. "Documenting the Olmsteds in Ohio." *Landscape Architecture* 77, no.5 (1987): pp.94-95.

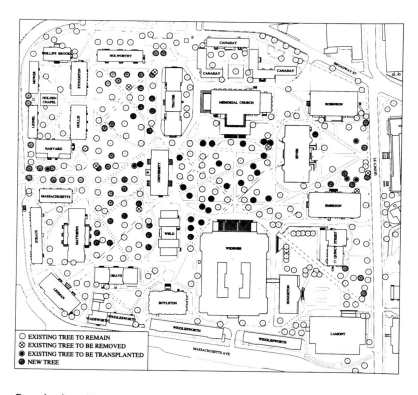

- ○ EXISTING TREE TO REMAIN
- ⊗ EXISTING TREE TO BE REMOVED
- ◉ EXISTING TREE TO BE TRANSPLANTED
- ● NEW TREE

See citation 476: Michael Van Valkenburgh and Peter Del Tredici. "Restoring the Harvard Yard Landscape." *Arnoldia*, 1994. Harvard Yard Tree replanting program, phase one work.

Role of the American Society of Landscape Architects (ASLA) state chapter and State Historic Planning Office (SHPO) in project. Methodology, financial and staff support; archival resource summary; national applications. illus.

480. Vernon, Noel Dorsey; Cairns, Malcolm. "Rehabilitation of a Woodland Park: Hills and Dales, Dayton." *CRM* 16, no.4 (1993): pp.26-28.

Research, documentation and evaluation of fifty-seven acre Ohio Olmsted Brothers woodland park. Treatment alternatives; public outreach and survey. bib., annotated. illus.

481. Vernon, Noel Dorsey; Garvey, C. Elizabeth; Williams, Sherda K. "Oral History Guidelines for Landscape Historians." Washington, D.C.: American Society of Landscape Architects Open Committee on Historic Preservation, 1990.

Types of projects. Organization, preparation, execution, and transcription. Ethical and legal considerations. bib., annotated

482. Visentini, Margherite Azzi; Scazzosi, Lionella. "The Conservation of Parks and Gardens in Italy." *Landscape Research* 12, no.2 (1987): pp.3-9.

Role of 1939 Statutes 1089 and 1497 protecting landscapes, objects and estates; 1981 International Charter for the Restoration of Historic Gardens (Florence Charter), treatment of stonework, grottos, discussed. Case studies from Padua, Trieste. illus.

483. Vogt-O'Connor, Diane. "Archival and Manuscript Materials at the NPS." *CRM* 17, no.5 (1994): pp.33-35.

Senior archivist, National Park Service Curatorial Services Division, describes agency's archival holdings, how materials are used, role of archivists. National Archives and Records Administrration (NARA), NPS-19 (Records Management Guideline), Collection Management Plans discussed.

484. von Baeyer, Edwinna. "A Selected Bibliography for Garden History in Canada." rev. ed. Canada: Canadian Heritage Parks, 1994.

Limited to designed landscapes, pre-1950 sources. Predominantly primary sources.

485. von Frese, Ralph R. B.; Noble, Vergil E. "Magnetometry for Archeological Exploration of Historical Sites." *Historical Archaeology* 18, no.2 (1984): pp.38-53.

Case study at Fort Ouiatenon, location of first european settlement in Indiana in the early eighteenth century, demonstrates use of magnetometer in locating cultural features such as hearths and wells, and establishing priorities in excavation strategy. bib. illus.

486. von Krosigk, Klaus. "International Conference Report: The Scenic Park: A Task for the Preservation of Historical Gardens, Berlin (West) June 26-June 29, 1989, Villa Borsig." *Landscape Research* 15, no.1 (1990): pp.29-30.

Conference resolutions on surrounding lands, partnerships, maintenance, training, outreach and international information exchange.

487. Wagner, Gail E. "Charcoal, Isotopes, and Shell Hoes: Reconstructing a 12th Century Native American Garden." *Expedition (The University Museum Magazine of Archaeology and Anthropology, University of Pennsylvania)* 32, no.2 (1990): pp.34-43.

Fort Ancient Indian Ohio settlement, SunWatch Village, excavated, added to National Register of Historic Places. Twelfth century corn and other vegetables researched, propagated, replanted. bib. illus.

488. Wainwright, Ian N. M. "Rock Painting and Petroglyph Recording in Canada." *APT Bulletin* 22, no.1&2 (1990): pp.55-84.

Methods and difficulties encountered in recording ancient art forms; focus on photographic techniques, digital image processing, tracing, rubbing, molding, casting and

stereophotogrammetry. National case studies include
Petroglyphs Provincial Park. bib. illus.

489. Wakefield, Mary M. B. "The Boston Public Garden:
Showcase of the City." *Arnoldia* 48, no.3 (1988): pp.32-47.

History, horticultural collection, decline, and late-twentieth
century restoration efforts of volunteer groups and city of
Boston. bib. illus.

490. Walter, Burke. "The Americans with Disabilities Act (ADA):
Compliance Solutions for Historic Buildings Using Landscape
Architecture." *Georgia Landscape* (1994): pp.2-3.

Background and overview. Challenges for historic
structures: balancing access requirements with visual impacts
(e.g. ramp solutions.) Benefits of regrading approaches.
Need for site-specific solutions.

491. Walters, William D., Jr. "The American Shale Paver: Its
Origin, Evolution, and Role in Landscape Preservation."
Pioneer American Society Transactions 10, (1987): pp.59-65.

Discussion of development of brick paver and its potential as
a unifying element in historic landscapes. bib. illus.

492. Walters, William C. "Partnerships in Parks and
Preservation." *Trends* 29, no.2 (1992): p.2.

Summary article for thematic issue, outgrowth of first
national conference on the subject, Albany, N.Y., September
1991. Protection of natural/cultural resources, providing
recreational opportunities.

493. Watson, A. Elizabeth. *Establishing An Easement Program to
Protect Historic, Scenic, and Natural Resources.*, National
Trust for Historic Preservation, Washington, D.C., 1992. 20
pp.

Easements: their purpose, how they work, legal
considerations, tax considerations, valuation, alternatives to
donated easements and organizing an easement program.
State-by-state legislation and list of selected easement holders.
bib.,annotated. illus.

494. Watson, John. "A Fountain Revived." *Landscape Design* no.208 (Mar.'92): pp.23-24.

Victorian gothic fountain from 1857 Plantation Garden in Norwich, U.K. restored. Documentation, restoration methods, accommodation to modern technology and environmental issues discussed. illus.

495. Watson, William C. "The Oregon-California Trails." *CRM* 16, no.11 (1993): pp.19-20.

Trail creation, inventory, preservation through public/private partnerships. Legislative overview. Forest service 'adopt-a-trail' program. National examples. illus.

496. Watts, Peter. "Australia's Historic Gardens Under Review." *APT Bulletin* 11, no.4 (1979): pp. 108-117.

Preliminary inventory of undocumented cultural resource; description of process including locating gardens, documentation, evaluation criteria, findings, complications, on-going efforts. Case study: Victoria. bib. illus.

497. Webb, Melody. "Cultural Landscapes in the National Park Service." *Public Historian* 9, no.2 (1987): pp.77-89.

Discusses need for management policy for vernacular landscapes under National Park Service (NPS) jurisdiction, recognizing needs of residents. Policy implications of 1966 National Historic Preservation Act; study resulting in "Cultural Landscapes: Rural Historic Districts in the National Park Service," Robert Melnick, 1984. bib.

498. Weeks, Kay. "Are We Losing Authenticity to Recover Appearances? Viewpoint Colloquy." *CRM* 17, no.5 (1994): pp.26-32.

Six preservation professionals offer views on restoration and reconstruction philosophy within and outside the National Park Service. Interpretation of cumulative historic layers versus a single period; relationships between treatment options and material authenticity discussed. illus.

499. Weeks, Kay. "The Ethical Implications of Starting a Collection." *CRM* 16, no.8 (1993): pp.26-27.

The principles embodied in the "Secretary of the Interior's Standards" in relationship to removing features from their contextual setting . Broad examples. illus.

500. Weinstein, Geraldine. "Replacing the Understory Plantings of Central Park." *Arnoldia* 45, no.2 (1985): pp.19-27.

The impacts of a century of depleted financial resources, misguided management, inadequate maintenance, and visitor impact. Contemporary approach based on history, growing conditions, use and management. Balancing aesthetic and ecological concerns. Case study: perimeter planting along Fifth Avenue between 72nd and 76th Streets (N.Y.C., N.Y.) to re-establish border. Methods for evaluating plants. illus.

501. Wescoat, James L., Jr.; Wolschke-Bulmahn, Joachim. "The Mughal Gardens of Lahore." *Die Gartenkunst* 6, no.1 (1994): pp.19-33.

History, significance of Mughal period gardens in Pakistan (1526-1759). Examples from city of Lahore; importance of water as structural and character-defining feature; twentieth century preservation planning; need for more legal protection, maintenance, discussed. bib. illus.

502. White, Bradford J.; Roddewig, Richard J. *Preparing a Historic Preservation Plan.*, American Planning Association, Chicago, Illinois, 1994. 58 pp.

Purpose, definitions, types and elements of a preservation plan. Preparation and implementation case studies: Kane County, Ill.; San Francisco, Calif.; Baltimore, Md.; Atlanta, Ga.; Iowa City, Iowa; Denver, Colo.; Lawrence, Kans. Appendices: Growth management laws; Secretary of the Interior's Standards; sample tools for evaluating significance, mission statements, action strategies and survey forms. Charts and tables. bib. illus.

503. Wilburn, Gary. *Routes of History: Recreational Use and Preservation of Historic Transportation Corridors.*, National Trust for Historic Preservation, Washington, D.C., 1985. 16 pp.

Discussion of types: canal, trail, rail road and highway.
Management and treatment issues associated with linear
resources. Case studies: Ill. and Mich. Canal National
Heritage Corridor; Patriot's Path, Morris County, N.J. and
Columbia River Scenic Highway, Oreg. Sources of assistance.
bib., annotated. illus.

504. Wilson, John S. "We've Got Thousands of These! What
Makes a Historic Farmstead Significant?" *Historical
Archaeology* 24, no.2 (1990): pp.23-33.

Consideration of individual farmstead sites within regional
context; relevance for selecting nominations on National
Register of Historic Places. Stepped screening process
recommended to maximize field work productivity in
determining significance of individual sites. Case study: Surry,
N.H. bib. illus.

505. Wilson, Patricia. "Historic Preservation and the
African-American Community: A Measure of Commitment to
Cultural Diversity." *CRM* 17, no.5 (1994): pp.21-25.

National Conference of State Historic Preservation Officers
(NCSHPO) attempts to increase African-American involvement
with historic preservation through new organizations,
networking, public awareness campaigns, professional
development programs. National examples. bib.

506. Wilson, Rex. *Archeology and Preservation.*, National Trust
for Historic Preservation, Washington, D.C., 1980. 20 pp.

Introduction to the discipline. Concepts and definitions.
Basic concepts: stratigraphy and sequence, ethnographic
analogy, cumulative change, environmental adaptation.
Analysis and intervention techniques. Planning
recommendations and sources of assistance. bib.

507. Wood, Christina D. "'A Most Dangerous Tree': The
Lombardy Poplar in Landscape Gardening." *Arnoldia* 54, no.1
(1994): pp.24-30.

Evolution of contemporary attitudes, landscape uses,
shortcomings of Lombardy Poplar (Populus nigra 'Italica').
illus.

508. Workman, John. "Restoration of Parklands and Subsequent Management." *Landscape Research* 7, no.1 (1982): pp.29-30.

   National Trust representative discusses U.K. parks and research objectives, management, maintenance strategies, including vegetation, tree surveys, water features, landforms, and associated costs.

509. Wright, John B. "Cultural Geography and Land Trusts in Colorado and Utah." *The Geographical Review* 83, no.3 (1993): pp.269-279.

   Local, regional land trust history. Impact of contemporary and settlement period cultural values on preservation decisions in Colorado and Utah. illus.

510. Wright, T. W. J. "Large Gardens and Parks: Maintenance, Management." London: Granada, 1982.

   Handbook on maintenance of large sites includes chapter on management of historic gardens.

511. Yaro, Robert D., ed. *New England Landscape: An Interdisciplinary Journal of Landscape Planning and Design* 1, no.1 (1988): 110 pp.

   First and only issue published. Preservation-related papers: Land Trusts: Innovations on an Old New England Idea, Gordon Abbott, Jr.; The Changing New England Landscape: A Sociodemographic History, A.E. Luloff; Conserving Special Landscapes: A Case Study of Block Island, Judith Benedict; Cross-Cultural Planning: Learning from the British Countryside, Richard W. Carbin. bib. illus.

512. Yentsch, Anne. "Historic Morven: the Archaeological Reappearance of an 18th Century Princeton Garden." *Expedition (the University Museum Magazine of Archaeology and Anthropology, University of Pennsylvania)* 32, no.2 (1990): pp.14-23.

   Study reveals two hundred year garden evolution at New Jersey site. Excavational archaeology, cartographic analysis, vegetation analysis (field survey, tree ring cores, phytolith analysis), management, funding discussed. bib. illus.

See citation 511: Robert D. Yaro, ed., *New England Landscape: An Interdisciplinary Journal of Landscape Planning and Design*, 1988. Atypical pre-development scene, with a rural village organically formed around a small nucleus of buildings including a farmstead, a church, and the town hall.

127

513. Zaitzevsky, Cynthia. "The Historian and the Landscape."
Historic Preservation Forum 7, no.3 (1993): pp.16-25.

Suggests new rigor and scholarship in research,
documentation of historic landscapes. Case studies: Augustus
Saint Gaudens National Historic Site (NHS), Cornish, N.H.;
Vanderbilt Mansion NHS, Hyde Park, N.Y.; Federick Law
Olmsted NHS, Brookline, Mass.; Dorchester Heights
Monument and Thomas Park, Boston, Mass.. bib. illus.

514. Zube, Ervin H.; Simcox, David E.; Law, Charles S.
"Perceptual Landscape Simulations: History and Prospect."
Landscape Journal 6, no.1 (1987): pp.62-82.

History, key research issues of static and dynamic visual
simulation. Effectiveness of multi-modal simulations;
importance of simulating landscape experiences. bib. illus.

515. Zwiech, Tomasz. "Civil War Battlefield Parks: An Inspiration
for Preservation in Poland." *CRM* 17, no.3 (1991): pp.11,17.

Potential application of treatment planning methodologies to
battlefields to Poland; techniques; inter-relationship of resource
values. bib.

516. Zwiech, Tomasz. "The Social Apects of Muskau Park in
Lecknica: Planning and Management in a Community
Context." *CRM* 17, no.7 (1994): pp.32-34.

History of park (1815-present). Preservation planning and
treatment inform interpretation. Author discussed "achieving a
balance between nature, culture, and spirit. Community
outreach programs increase pride, care of resource. bib. illus.

Subject Index

SUBJECT INDEX

Subject Index

Making Educated Decisions

Geographic Index

GEOGRAPHIC INDEX

Norwich, 494
Peak District: 15
Rousham, 333
Sheffield, 200
Suffolk, 189
Sussex, 420
West London, 218
West Penwith, 389
Wiltshire, 5
York, 171
Yorkshire, 265, 340
Scotland: 373
Scotland: Edinburgh, 210
Wales: 6, 57, 104
United States:
Alabama:
Birmingham, 203
Mobile, 443
Montgomery, 449
Selma, 449
Alaska: 271
Arizona: 56, 82
Canyon de Chelly, 95, 462
California: 102, 155, 185
Big Sur, 440
Danville, 162
Long Beach, 44, 302, 415, 444
Martinez, 121
Oakland, 430
Sacramento, 430
San Francisco, 141, 399, 502
Walnut Creek, 468
Colorado: 56, 509
Mesa Verde, 212
Connecticut: 440
Fairfield City, 263
Guilford, 440
Stamford, 262
Delaware: 467
Wilmington, 7

Florida: 56
St. Augustine, 1, 256
Georgia: 84
Piedmont, 134
Savannah, 1, 77
Hawaii:
Hanalei, 440
Kauai, 325
Idaho: 102
Illinois: 308
Bloomington, 491
Chicago, 39, 428
Kane County, 502
Lakeside, 429
McHenry County, 440
Mount Carroll, 98
Riverside, 70
Springfield, 39, 187
Vandalia, 236
Indiana:
Fort Quiatenon, 485
Terre Haute, 236
Iowa:
Ames, 189
Dubuque County, 440
Iowa City, 502
Plumb Grove, 188
Kansas: 234
Farlington, 112
Nicodemus, 145
Kentucky:
Cranks, 440
Hardin County, 440
Middlesboro, 440
Lousiana: 150, 471, 472
New Iberia, 302, 411, 498
New Orleans, 297, 467
Maine:
Mt. Desert Island, 302
Wells, 440
Maryland: 377, 467
Annapolis, 450

Author Index

AUTHOR INDEX

Author Index

Making Educated Decisions

☆ U.S. GOVERNMENT PRINTING OFFICE: 1994 381-917/20273